LET YOUR FRAZZLE
BE YOUR DAZZLE

Finding The Spiritual Magic In Your Life

Lillie Ruby

Lillie Ruby Creatives

This book is dedicated to family and friends who have stood beside me, checked in on me, pulled me up off the curb, pushed me down the road and loved me openly so that I didn't give up in times of despair and confusion.
It is also dedicated to my spiritual teachers who have led me to deeper ways of thinking and doing. Some are famous, most are not. Some, only I can see. Each of you has been important to my life.
Thank you for loving, guiding and supporting me.

The brighter the light, the darker the shadow.

CARL JUNG

CONTENTS

PREFACE

It was another hot July, and I was attending an international virtual event with over three thousand participants. We were working with the energies that flow through our bodies. The event's intent was to emphasize that the energies flowing through us are bigger and more expansive than the typical binding description of  chakra and are actually the energies of how we function in life. Little did I know, by the end of the event, I would see an activity, in which we participated, tie into messages I had been receiving for quite a while from that enormous University in the sky.

The study of each energy followed an instructional order. First, we heard a lecture and then participated in a meditation about that particular energy. Next, we drew an oracle card and used the card's imagery as a trigger to journal about the energy. We recorded any intuitive messages we received. That was all followed by a break-out session to share our aha's with other attendees we had never met.

We were asked to share in those small groups as the responses from other participants to the intuitive hits could be revealing. It often lay your heart open and allowed for deeper reflection.

In my first journaling session, I drew a card. I opened my spiritual heart and ears and heard something that made me laugh, "Allow the frazzle to be your dazzle." I knew immediately that this phrase tagged onto other spiritual messages I had been receiving over the past few months, and actually a few times in years past. I also realized my oral messenger had just provided me with a phrase that was also a snappy book title if I ever heard one.

It was a simple start for this book. It may sound easy, but it also took days, weeks, and months, well no, years of asking, "What would you have me do?"

I had thought I needed to achieve some level of skill and accomplishment, or be pointed in a specific direction. I was seeking my own way, but doubting at the same time. I didn't understand my confusion or how to break free from such a circular and frustrating way of existing.

After some time, I began to realize I couldn't make a commitment to any of it, or myself, because I was actually conflicted. Conflicted about betraying my family's and community's behaviors and values versus betraying myself and what I was learning through life and my spiritual connections. I was conditioned that telling the truth would bring punishment, not love. I also knew from experience, that people would hastily exit your life if you revealed anything about abuse. Until I realized what the quandary I was experiencing, I struggled with allowing Spirit, God, the Universe, or whatever term you may use, have free reign in my life.

After hearing, "Let your frazzle be your dazzle," I began to take another look at my life. I found that no matter what suffering or fear there had been, the Spiritual world have been walking beside me and providing all types of experiences to show me it was there. I hope my story, not only entertains you, but encourages you to look at your life differently, too.

INTRODUCTION

As you've read, I had been fighting the idea of writing my story for several years. I fought against the idea even when an instructor in a mediumship class turned to me and said, "Your guides are saying you have to tell your story! Then she added rather matter-of-factly, "Your allergic to nuts."

I didn't want to hear either message. I whined, "I don't want to tell what all happened. There are too many victim stories out there already. No one would want to read my story. I've worked too hard to move beyond it. The people who need to know probably wouldn't believe me." Followed by, "What? That can't be! I love nuts. I eat them all the time."

Guess who was right, me or my spiritual guides? I stopped eating nuts and much to my dismay, my life-long sinus issues improved dramatically. I was sad to say goodbye to nuts, but I did.

It has been hard, though. Native pecan trees grow everywhere around where I live. They are a staple in nearly all baked goods during community events. Meat is smoked with pecan tree wood. I haven't met a pecan recipe I didn't like, either. I guess, though, breathing is a little more important, but that book? I didn't think I needed to breathe deeply that badly. Some things are just hard to get off your chest.

Spirit was metaphorically beating down my heart's door trying to get me writing, but still I resisted. After a few more years, I took my fingers out of my ears, listened, and started writing. I have included some of the painful things because they mattered, but I tried not to horrible-ize. The truth needed to brought into the light to disarm it, and in some cases, celebrate it. My story didn't have to be perfect, regardless of what Chatty Cathy, my name for my smack-talking mind, said. I'm not listening to her any more. I have evicted her from her home in my head.

You will find that my story wanders across time, but that is part of the point. I'll admit, I dragged my feet adding to the length of the time line, but that's also how it became a life's story rather than a random event story.

Spirit didn't work in straight lines in my life, or wait for me to achieve perfection. I didn't just wake up one day with the Universe applauding while everything fell in place. There was no cosmic explosion. I slowly developed a special awareness of my place in this Universe.

I know there are people who won't like the information I'm about to reveal. There are people who won't believe it. That doesn't matter as long as it's the truth. In the middle of editing the information and to emphasis the importance of telling this story, a confirmation was gifted to me. My mother's spirit came through the day before her birthday. She had this to say, "...I'm glad you are writing about your life although it's hard to read. What I did was wrong. I was wrong about so many things..." At the same moment, Archangel Uriel was standing beside me. He is known as Angel of Truth and Transformation.

So, I have included some of the challenging parts of my life, but it has not been my focus. Instead, I have focused on the wacky, crazy, miraculous ways God has shown up in my life, even during some of the painful times, and helped me create a dazzling me.

I

I traveled in this or that direction for a while with my spiritual development. Maybe I got distracted by a new shiny tool, or someone convinced me to attend a class on something I knew nothing about. It could have been I was just bored and looking for something new to experience. Sometimes, something new/ strange happened. Instead of trusting what was right in front of my face or whispering in my ears, I kept waiting for that cosmic movie screen (cue music) to light up and tell me exactly what to do and who I was.

Growing more confused over the years, I never knew if I should wear shoes to build up energy or go barefoot to drain energy into the earth. Should I look right-side up or upside down? Would a job be better for consistency or should I build a business? What are my skills? Am I even supposed to use them for anything? Maybe I made some secret pact with a demon? I was sure I had not! Maybe, I just wasn't supposed to help anyone with my skills, but yet, people always seemed to show up. I was moving about my life, willy-nilly, because I couldn't understand the plan, if there was one. I just knew I couldn't quite lean into an idea that represented a "normal" life. So, I kept searching.

At one point I even got off track and began collecting what I considered spiritual decorations. That came from a childhood need to be/look "right," if I was to be loved. The items weren't necessarily something I really wanted, but something I thought might make me, "look better; more acceptable."

Spirit drew me up short one day, though. My home was burglarized by a neighborhood gang while I went to lunch with a friend. What they stole was a few crystals and my spiritual decorations.

They did leave a television after they dropped it. Busted communication, hmmmm. More on communication later.

It seemed like an odd cache to steal until my daughter pointed out I had started trying to *look* spiritual. I immediately realized she was right. I had briefly fallen off the spirituality wagon and I have never forgotten that lesson.

Spirituality isn't about the doodads and statues, or what clothes you wear. It isn't about buildings, schedules, candles or singing. It's about truth and harmony with the Universe and that Great Creator. I understood Spirit's point after my collection was stolen.

I'm reminded of that stunning lesson when I see others in costumes, and doing whatever they believe will convince people they are of the highest levels of spirituality. I don't offer that as a judgement. Lessons come in all kinds of ways. Those people are simply reminders for me to stick with what is right for me.

I have no doubt now. Although I may wander with what I do or learn, it's still about Spirit. It's animism. It's not about humanness, and it's certainly not about decorations or clothing. It's ok to wear jeans and a t-shirt or a flowy blouse that makes me feel like a fairy. It's okay to walk about with a giant crystal hanging from my neck because it makes me feel lovely and protected. It's also ok to have spiritual decorations as long as they mean something to me.

I began to live in ways that felt more aligned with the authentic me, regardless of the looks or comments I received. That's how I began to light my frazzle to the point of being dazzling. Getting to this point certainly wasn't easy. There were many epiphanies and challenges along the way. There is a lot of judgement against anyone who thinks, or knows, there might be more to this life than what convention dictates. It's wasn't as simple as it sounds though. Conditioning can be a hard task master.

II

Over the years, my life started to look like the back side of a hurricane. That type of storm builds up energy trying to get somewhere. Most everything it sucks up; it then throws out the backside. After it has passed by your house, there is a bunch of random stuff scattered around that you still need to put into piles and figure out what to do with it all. That stuff may not be a thing from your house or property. That stuff may have come from who knows where. It still has to be cleaned up and sense made of it all. Well, at least I felt like I had to make sense of it all, but that was from conditioning during my childhood.

I ended up unnecessarily carrying a lot of baggage. I was often the clean-up person in my family. I was regularly required to take care of someone, all older than me, or to cover for someone. If someone was upset, I had to take care of it, or take on work beyond my years to try and make that person happy. I was well trained to be the overly responsible and an overly used scape goat. I lived in a perpetual whirlwind of, "If ____ isn't happy, ain't nobody happy." It seemed no one was ever happy, but they were satisfied to point blame or responsibility in my direction.

Eventually, I willfully took on persona of the overly responsible in hopes of finding that sweet spot of love. I wanted to be a good girl. I wanted to be loved. I wanted to be special to someone. I really didn't know how to accomplish those basic security goals without sacrificing myself. I didn't know how to step back and let others give to me, not even God. I ended up as the over-achiever, the over doer- and the over-giver, not the unconditionally loved. I ended up depressed and perpetually exhausted, mentally, emotionally, physically and spiritually.

What I did know was that there was something greater than what I had been taught or I felt I had accomplished. That's why I was wandering about trying to find that something greater and feeling very frazzled. Spirit was with me, though, and the Universe had my back whether or not I realized it at the time.

I experienced times of obvious protection like the rainy night in Alabama. I was driving on our long trip home to Georgia from Christmas in Texas. The roads were slick. The kids were very tired and cranky. We literally forced them to put on their seat belts. As I drove along, I was in the second lane from the inside of a multi-laned interstate highway. My attention was captured by a car that stopped in the inside lane. Theoretically, I shouldn't have seen that car from as far away as I did. When you're under angelic wings of protection, things like that, and like what else have transpired, happen.

There were two cars approaching from behind the car that had just stopped. I knew there was the potential of a serious accident. I hit the brake because I knew those other two cars would probably react by pulling into my lane, possibly without looking for other cars. The road was slick. As I hit my brake, so did the other two drivers, while also pulling into my lane. Everything went into slow motion. All three cars spun out in different directions that should have made us all collide. We spun across the entire freeway without hitting the car that stopped or each other. I still remember seeing their faces as we spun around each other. The van ended up so close to rolling off a large overpass that there was no room for me to step trembling out of the van. That small strip of dirt stopped the slide of the van and kept my family from tumbling down the overpass.

No one in the three cars was hurt, but the kids were crying and dangling upside down from their seat belts. Thank goodness we made them put the belts on. We were facing the wrong way and into oncoming traffic.

I could see that the traffic that had been all around us was now at least a quarter of a mile back. I could see all the headlights, but no one was around us while we all got turned around. When the impossible happens, you know your angels were taking care of their assigned duty.

That night was New Year's Eve. I had a new awareness for the coming year. Our angels had protected all of us. Even the person who had caused the near accident was unharmed.

I was involved in another freeway incident in another state. My van slid right up to the driver's door of a car turned sideways from an accident. I had managed to stop my van in an impossibly short distance. The horrific look on the man's face through that car window, who probably thought I might hit and kill him, was awful. By then, I had learned a few things about the Universe, so as I pressed the brake pedal with both feet. I screamed as loud as I could to the van that weighed over 6000 pounds, "STOP. STOP. STOP." I yelled over and over, as intensely as I could, until I made that impossible stop. I went from going 70 miles per hour to nothing in just a few yards. I slid up to that car, but stopped a couple of feet away. I knew I had help with that, but we can do miraculous things when we call for help.

Another time I received spiritual protection; I was headed to Target to get some supplies. I kept losing my keys. After 3-4 times of impossibly losing my keys as I tried to walk out the door, I decided maybe my guides didn't want me to go to Target. I gave up and turned on my computer to check email.

Up popped an email asking if I was ok. "Yes, I'm okay," I replied. I continued, "Why do you ask?" My future daughter-in-law replied she had just seen breaking news that there was a shooter in my city that had killed four people.

I turned on the television and found out why I kept losing my keys that morning. A breaking news story stated that the shooter killed those people right in the part of the mall's parking lot where I always parked. Most people didn't use that side entrance. It was the back entrance into Target. The next day's newspaper included this paraphrased information:

Man kills neighbor, steals car, stopped by police officer, shoots officer, car chase to the mall, shooter kills two more in mall parking lot, kills officer inside Target and wounds several shoppers in the store.

After the first traffic stop and shooting of a police officer, there was a car chase to the mall. The streets traveled during the car chase were a few blocks from my house. It's possible, that while traveling to Target, I could have ended up in the middle of that car chase and been injured. My spiritual guides were protecting me by hiding my keys so I wouldn't be in my car as these horrific events took place.

My spiritual protectors have used keys several times to keep me away from something, but I don't always know what it might be. It's clear my guides see keys as more than pieces of metal to stick into the car's ignition. They are also messages and tools for protection.

A teenager from a couple of streets away was systematically breaking into neighbors' homes while they were at work. This particular day, he had targeted my home.

We had experienced a bad ice storm in the city. The place where I worked was closed due to the weather. So, I was home from work the day he decided to break into my house.

I heard glass crash in the basement and went to investigate. I found the burglar gathering up my things in a plastic bag to steal. In my anger, I did everything that day you aren't supposed to do. The burglar ended up running away from me. I'm sure Spirit protected me the next time he apparently came back, too.

I had a pesky grape vine that loved to grow in and around my chain link fence. It frequently draped long tendrils over the fence that seemed to grow overnight. Sometimes, they dangled over the driveway that was just a couple of feet away from the fence.

A couple of weeks after the burglary, I came home from work. As I was pulling into the driveway, something caught my eye. There, hanging from a curled grape vine tendril, was a huge set of various standard house keys. There must have been thirty keys on that ring. I don't know how the vine held the weight, but grape vines are strong enough to make furniture. The ring of keys was bobbing up and down in the breeze and out hanging over the edge of the driveway. I couldn't miss them. I actually had to stop the car, to get out and move the keys so they wouldn't bang against my windshield. I knew the burglar had come back, but had lost his keys.

I don't know who hung them from the grape vine. I doubt the vine snatched them from the burglar's pocket as he walked by. That many keys wouldn't have fit easily into a back pocket. I had to uncurl the grape vine tendril to release them. It was as though they had been threaded onto that curly tendril. None of my neighbors knew anything about the set of keys. I'm sure you realize what I am about to say, "It was clearly impossible for that to have happened." It did, though. I knew I had been spiritually protected once again.

I believe those keys were hung there so I would find them and know, not only that the burglar had come back, but that I had been spiritually protected. (By the way, he was captured a couple of weeks later when he tried to break into my neighbor's house while she was in the hospital.)

I had no idea why I was delayed from driving this next time. I still don't. By the time the following event happened, I had long since learned to accept there would be a reason my keys were MIA. If keys were involved, I needed to pay attention. Being saved from the mall shooter and the sight of those keys bobbing in the air from the grape vine were engraved in my memory.

I was dressed and ready to go to work. I couldn't find my keys. They weren't in their usual place. I began to search the house. No luck. I searched my room and the house several times. No luck. I dumped my purse contents out several times and searched the lining. No luck. I was pretty frustrated by that time.

My mom got up and asked why I was still home. She began the search too. She searched the house and my room several times. She dumped my purse out more than once, too. We felt around in the lining. We turned the lining inside out several times. The keys weren't hanging from the ignition, so I hadn't locked them in my car.

After another twenty minutes, or so, of Mom and I both looking everywhere, even the places we knew my keys wouldn't be, I gave up. I said, "Well, I guess I will have to call in. I can't imagine what has happened to my keys."

As I went to make the phone call about 45 minutes after I started my search, I felt a mental nudge. I decided, against all logic, to look in my purse one more time. I opened my purse and called to mom to come look. There, right on top of everything, were my keys.

I still don't know what I might have been saved from that day, but it was clear Spirit had been delaying me leaving the house. There was no way in the physical world those keys could have ended up right on top of my wallet and other stuff in my purse. I had been delayed nearly an hour for some reason. I've never questioned it, but I still wonder what I was protected from that day.

III

Even though I had some pretty dramatic examples of spiritual protection under my belt, it was me I couldn't quite wrap my head around. I felt a desperate pull to be something I didn't think I was. I wasn't sure I could even be whatever *that* was. I thought I had to do/learn everything myself, and figure it out all on my own. That was psychological conditioning from childhood, but it continued to affect my adulthood.

I felt I was frazzling more each day. I was trying to figure out what I was supposed to be. I worked hard, but took some missteps. I wasn't being true to myself. I could feel that, but I wasn't sure how to be true to myself, as I had never been allowed to truly be myself. I didn't know who I was.

Some of the events of my childhood left me with deep abandonment issues. I've struggled with that in relationships and even with God and my spiritual development. On the days when my spiritual interaction was quiet, or I had connection issues because of interference from my low self-worth, it was easy to slip into that abandoned mode and give up.

I became a collector of ways to do things. Since I later needed certifications for massage therapy licensing, that seemed ok. What I studied wasn't questioned as it might have been, at least with strangers. It was a place to hide the real me until one day, I realized all those certifications were just pieces of paper, not my value as a person.

Those classes and books simply weren't providing me all I was seeking. I just didn't know what I was really seeking. I had an increasingly large bag of tricks, but I was no closer to figuring out how to be the *one* thing that I thought I was supposed to be, or what that looked like.

To add to the frustration, I was tip-toeing around. If I had owned an invisibility cloak, I would have worn it. Not many knew who I really was, especially family. It was a safety feature that sometimes worked, sometimes didn't. I still got plenty of strange looks, eye rolls and people leaving my life. Eventually, I learned that I was simply betraying myself by not being open about my beliefs and experiences, but there was plenty of heart ache before that realization.

Even in the 21st Century, there are still people who cry, "Witch!" and expect the community to attack someone simply because that person's beliefs look or sound different. It doesn't matter whether that person's beliefs or actions actually *are* different or if there are any facts. Truth doesn't play a role in this type of behavior.

This type of behavior is actually known as horizontal violence. It is a way to bully and haze another person through any number of ways including, talking behind a person's back, ignoring them, sarcastic comments, slamming things, starting rumors or covertly encouraging others to take action against a person to gain power and control over the victim. It harms, disrespects, and devalues the worth of the recipient and is certainly spiritually damaging. It's still hard to wrap my head around adults behaving that way, but it's what happened to me.

Let me add here, I have nothing against anyone practicing the craft. As far as I'm concerned, it's another way to work with the energy of the Universe. That energy is provided to us by God, is us, and is everything. Even the Field of Science now agrees that we are mostly vibrating energy. I bet God said, "Finally!" when that was announced!

I witnessed a natural occurrence that duplicated what I had read about how a coven of people increase energy. I am gifted at picking up on patterns, but if I hadn't read about working energy this way, I wouldn't have recognized it.

I took my mom to a monthly luncheon with her Sunday School class members. They sat in a circle. The ladies brought birthday cards for each person with a birthday that month. The birthday celebrants began opening and reading their cards. After they were read and admired, each birthday celebrant expressed gratitude for the card. Each card was then passed clockwise to the next person. Around and around these cards went, pouring energy and good wishes into the center of the circle. The ladies began to be more and more animated as the energy built. They began to laugh more and more while building the energy. About that time, it hit me. There were thirteen woman in that circle. Covens are said to use thirteen people to increase energy. They had no idea what they were doing, other than having a great time, but it showed me that it was a natural phenomenon, not something wicked or evil.

The energy from the Universe can be applied in good or bad ways in all circumstances, just like in the Sunday School luncheon. In my case, a woman decided to brand me a bad person, unworthy of working or living in "her community" because first, she allowed herself to be manipulated, secondly, she wasn't interested in finding out the truth, and thirdly, because she was a willing participant in horizonal violence.

The woman had never met me, but formed opinions about me and took actions against me. Those actions included attempting to get me fired and driven out of the community. That all came about because she was told I had written and published an article about rocks. Rocks? Yes, rocks!

This attack came from someone I, long ago, had started calling Little c christians. By that, I mean people who, in my opinion, are on a power trip rather than following any religious teaching I've read. It certainly isn't what I believe the behavior of a true Christian with a capitol C should be.

Why do I apply this term to the woman trying to get me fired? I found out she was in church most Sundays, but yet, she was trying to damage my life when she wasn't in church. For me, that's a Little c.

I've encountered the Little c's in many different places in the community and at various places I've worked. I've encountered them when they had no idea what my view of God/Spirit might be, just like the lady who tried to get me fired.

Commonly, I find they try to control and bully people and businesses by whatever misguided ideology they may have absorbed. It's really a power and authority issue. It's horizontal violence, more than it is about God, Christianity, or Spirituality. Here are some other examples from my life encounters with the sort of person I call a Little c.

I answered the phone at a friend's office one day. She is a chiropractor. The lady calling the office demanded to know if I was a Christian. "Pardon?" I asked. The lady then went on a rant about how she can't do business with the chiropractor if she isn't a Christian. Since I hesitated to answer, clearly, she decided, I wasn't a Christian and it must not be a Christian business.

I tried to explain. I was just helping a friend in the office. Her question had taken me by surprise, but she had made up her mind from my response. As her final note, she added that her minister had told them not to do business with non-Christians.

She made a decision about my friend's chiropractic clinic without one shred of evidence. I wondered if she hadn't called just to create that drama and to have a story to tell the next Sunday.

That, of course, is just one example of how I came up with the term Little c christian. That lady was all about judging and condemning people without allowing any rebuttal. As far as I am concerned, she didn't fit my version of what living a Spiritual, much less Christian life, looked like.

Even after experiences like the one in my friend's office, I was still a bit gob smacked, when years later, I read an email at my new place of work. I felt like I had stepped through a worm hole and back several centuries.

I actually saw an email telling my brand new boss I should be fired. The lady writing the email somehow found out that I had written and published articles online about crystals, the rocks I mentioned earlier. This person actually wrote, "We don't want people like her in the community."

As I stared at that email, I felt flabbergasted. "This person has an issue with me writing about rocks?" I thought. Also thinking, "Why is someone snooping into my life in the first place? Why does she think she has anything to say about my life? How does she know I have been publishing articles online? How does she

14

know I was hired just yesterday? Who is this person? Why does she think she has a right to destroy my life? Is this Salem, Massachusetts or the Inquisition? What century is this?"

There is some irony to this. I live in a state where gas and oil income butters nearly every household's bread. Nearly every rock you turn over (pun intended) has a geologist lurking under it. Geology is very important to the area's economy. I even spent half my childhood living in company housing in a gas production plant. It should not have come as such a shock that I took geology in college and developed a love for rocks Why she would consider it an evil pasttime is the question.

It turned out my brother, was behind the woman's accusations and subsequent actions. It turned out he was also behind other deliberate misinformation that has been cast about the community. Apparently, my brother convinced the lady to write to my new boss and ask that I be fired. However, she was a willing participant in horizontal violence and responsible for her own actions. She didn't have to follow his lead.

Regardless, it seemed to be a prevailing attitude in the community. There was a stranger in their midst, even though my family had lived there for decades. Whenever someone doesn't fit the prevailing script, that person can be considered a danger. Accepting someone new may require a person to take action within themselves, and to change who they are. For some people, it's just easier to attack someone than to make changes.

My brother simply fanned the smoldering embers of some very narrow-minded thinking. I thought the history of our culture had cured that type of thinking. I was very wrong and shocked. Horizontal violence seemed to be all around me. I wasn't used to that.

In addition to the obvious manipulation and horizontal violence, I'm sure many of you understand what was happening. When you are the real dazzling you, what you may not hear is, "Way to go. Put yourself out there. Be real. Be authentic. Be happy."

Apparently, no one thought to ask, "You must have taken some geology classes. Is that why you love crystals?" "Tell me about crystals, etc." No one ever asked me if any of what was said was actually true, or what might have motivated such a mean, destructive behavior. It was a perplexing turn of events for me. I later asked Dad, "Why does he (my brother) have to be so mean?" Dad's reply was, "He's jealous." "Of what?" I asked. Dad shrugged and said, "I'm just telling you that's what it is. He is jealous."

I later learned that many people considered my brother a hothead and a bully. No one wanted to deal with him. Many of the community members apparently went along with whatever he said or did simply for self-preservation. That's a sad commentary on some of the community, but I suppose they can't help being who they are any more than I can. While working in the field of domestic violence, I had learned, people will surprise you with what they will do, or accept, to preserve their safety. I certainly saw it in action in my family.

Although I had never been attacked like before, when you are different, as I have always been, you get used to most of it, *the look*, the eye rolls. It doesn't necessarily have anything to do with religion. That sort of thing happened to students who studied music and drama in college. I know, I was a student in that department.

Judgmental behavior derives from limited thinking and/or exposure to new ideas, laced with a heavy dose of the fear of not being enough. The person being judged doesn't have to be threatening for the rejection to occur. There is no excuse for that behavior. It can leave a person in a state of turmoil, though. Rejection for no real reason, other than just being yourself is painful.

I'd gone to a friend's house. He asked what I had been doing. I excitedly began reviewing the talking points of a quantum psychics symposium I had been watching. He shut me down because I was, "Throwing out bunch of big words." Even though that was his issue, the rejection of being myself hurt.

After I returned to my home area to live, I even had a former classmate say, "We sat in the same Sunday School. What happened to you?" She was distracted by another person so I never had the opportunity to say, "My view of God, the Universe and our souls expanded!"

The rejection didn't come just from "those" people however. There is a lot of rejection in other genres, too. When you are different even in a "different" world it happens there too.

I attended a class online. I don't remember the topic, but it was something about using your intuition. We chatted a bit before beginning. The instructor addressed me saying, "Your voice is deeper than most women's voice." She actually physically shuddered before adding, "I *think* I can work with you though." I couldn't believe it. I was being rejected because God put me in the alto section of the choir. It was supposed to be a spiritually based class. I didn't hang around to hear more. There are biases in that world too.

IV

As I worked with energy fields for healing, my energy fields grew in strength and expanded. You will read, later, about how I became aware of healing energy. While it was a good thing to improve the flow of energy through and around me, sometimes it had unexpected results, and sometimes pretty funny results, too.

I hadn't really realized my energy fields were expanding and growing stronger. I did notice that when I walked into a restaurant or a meeting people stopped and looked at me. I didn't know it was because my energy field hit them. I didn't pay much attention other than to note the phenomenon.

While I worked at a domestic violence shelter, I was required to meet weekly with my up line. One day, she shocked me by saying something about me being intimidating. I stared at her and then replied, "I don't try to intimidate anyone!" Her reply was, "I know that *now!*" She continued with, "You are so accustomed to walking into your program rooms with authority, you don't realize how intimidating you can be."

I really had to process that idea. I couldn't see where I ever walked into a meeting with intimidation because that wasn't my intention.

I finally realized it was the strong energy fields around me. People weren't used to encountering strong fields except from people of authority, so that's how they filtered the vibration from me. It was about how they filtered the energy, not what I was doing.

Before I had walked the Prairie Labyrinth for the first time, (More on the labyrinth later.) my energy field was measured by using dowsing rods. Most of the participants, that day, had the expected four to six feet of energy field around them. Mine measured out at about ten feet. After we walked the labyrinth our fields were measured again. When I got to the barbed wire fence across the road, the instructor said, "Just come back. I can't measure how much your field expanded."

Reactions to my energy field created some funny incidents, too.

I worked concessions at the stadiums in Kansas City, MO for a non-profit group that raised money for education. One Sunday before a Chiefs game began, I set up all the cash drawers in our stand and helped with whatever else needed to be done. Afterward, I started walking down the concourse to use the restroom before the gates opened.

We always had a couple dozen law enforcement officers around the stands. I knew many of them because I was usually in charge of the concession stand's money. They made sure we were well protected.

Right before the football games started, the officers had an organizational meeting beside the restrooms. This morning, there must have been a new group of officers as they did rotate that special duty.

As I approached the pre-game meeting, I receive an energetic visual that cracked me up. I guess some of them recognized me because not all of them responded to my energy in this way, but at least a dozen did.

I saw what looked like energetic periscopes that popped up several feet over the officers' heads. The periscopes started tracking me. As I walked closer most of the energetic periscopes dropped, but a couple continued to track me as I walked past. One was still up and waiting for me when I walked back by the meeting. It tracked me as I returned to the stand, laughing.

I knew many members of the law enforcement community were sensitive to energy. Their lives depend upon it. That profession, more any other, would simply nod in understanding if I mentioned I could feel energy off people. They usually didn't give me that "look." I wasn't really surprised they responded to my energy, but it was a funny experience.

I was selling margaritas along side a man name Ed during a KC Royals game. He is deaf. I used very primative sign language to communication with him, but Ed was very good at figuring out what I was saying to him.

I caught Ed's attention, tapped my nose and made rain with my fingers. He looked askanced at me and shook his head. I nodded my head and repeated my signing that I smelled rain. He looked at me again. I made my signs again. Ed walked out on the concourse so he had a full view of the sky. He shook his head at me. I make the, I smell rain signs again. He responded by circling his finger around his ear, telling me I was crazy. There wasn't a cloud in the sky, no wind, in fact it was a beautiful afternoon for a baseball game. The game ended and we began to clean up the concession stand when a huge clap of thunder sounded and it began to pour rain. It rained so hard, we were soaked to the skin. How I smelled rain nearly 4 hours away I have no idea, but I believe it was a case of clairalience. I've had it happen a few times, like smelling someone smoking who isn't present or smelling birthday cake on a friend's breath while talking to him on the phone (He had just eaten a slice of cake.)

The evening scheduled Royals baseball games could last until late at night. By the time I counted money, we completed inventory, and we got the concession stand cleaned up, it could be pretty late, or early in the morning. It wasn't unusual to see a police car following me, at a distance, as I drove away from the stadium through some rougher sections of the city.

One particular night, however, I guess I was in full SLIder mode. (Street Light Interference). As I drove along a long empty boulevard, I noted the police car behind me. I also noticed that as I drove by, the street lights were going out one by one. I knew it was from my energy.

The funny thing about it was, as each light went out, the police car behind me got slower and slower. I watched in my rearview mirror as they dropped back further and further from my car. I'm sure they were trying to figure out what the heck was going on, with the lights blinking out at steady intervals.

Another night, I arrived at home with groceries. As got out of my car, the street light turned off. While I took some groceries into the house, it came back on. It went off again three or four times as I walked out of the house. It then came back on each time I went into the house. The street light finally gave up and was sputtering, not knowing if the sun was up, or if the sun had set.

Traveling home for holidays was a long, lonely and nearly 900 miles trip. One Christmas season, I was entertaining myself during the trip by doing various energy activities and exercises to expand my consciousness.

I stopped at the half-way point for a short visit with my son. It was around dusk when I pulled up to the stop light right beside a water feature. It was in front of a subdivision entry way. I looked over to enjoy the fountain. It turned off. I thought, "Oh, it must be timed to turn off at dusk." I started to turn my attention back to the stop light, when the fountain came back on. I turned to look at the fountain again, but it turned off. I realized I was the culprit. I looked back and forth a couple more times turning the fountain off and on and laughing. Obviously, it had a light sensor that turned it off or on and it was sensing my energy field. The people in cars behind me probably thought that water feature had lost its mind.

While I've had other pretty hilarious things happen, it's not so funny when the energy messes up a computer or cell phone. It all plays a part, though, in turning all of the frazzled experiences of my life into dazzle.

V

I was still struggling with the idea of writing a book about my life. During a meditation I saw a whole stack of books on a table. They were all written by me. A couple of years went by. Occasionally, I tried to start writing a book, but I still have some work to do if I'm going to produce that stack of books.

I even invested in a "Write a Book in a Weekend" seminar, but it was a bust. The second day of the seminar was my dad's birthday, and a little over a year after he passed. That weekend brought up a lot of the stuff from my life, but a book to publish wasn't one of them. I was surprised that I didn't end the weekend with a book as promised, but not completely.

During the latter part of the second day of the seminar, the instructor pulled me from the class and out into the front hallway of the Unity Church Pyramid. He handed me a large sheet of paper and pen. He requested that I write answers to a few questions he asked. I never finished the answers because he interrupted me saying, "You *can* write! You are writing your answers as stories." He then pointed out to me exactly how I was writing stories. I never told him about a life event, but he ended with, "Who told you, you couldn't write?"

Well, that ended the day for me as I burst into tears. I knew it was about Dad and my kindergarten experience. You will read more about that later. I spent most of the rest of the day with my hands in the church's outdoor water feature letting the movement of the water pull painful energy away through my hands and wash away my tears.

Even though, I was writing for a newspaper, that doubt about my ability to write was still firmly in place. Yet, I had so much spiritual drive in me, it just couldn't be contained. While I might not be writing my story, I was constantly creating and writing something through my job. The owner of the newspaper frequently commented on my creativity.

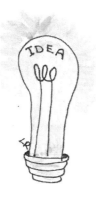

Being highly creative wasn't a new thing for me. I was used to the wide-eyed looks of people not wired so randomly as I. When my creative juices were really flowing, I might see people staring at me from slack-jawed faces. I often heard, "How do you come up with this stuff?" Not many people ever really "got me." Honestly, not even me, because I didn't know how I came up with stuff. I just knew I could.

I do remember the day I publicly accepted that part of myself, though. During a staff training, I told the Director of the domestic violence shelter where I worked, "If you need ideas, I can come up with them." When she questioned, "Really?" I was firm and, for me, brave. I repeated, "Yes. If you need ideas, I'm your person. I'm really good at coming up with ideas." Yet, I didn't fully recognize that I was channeling those ideas and co-creating with Spirit.

Writing and oral communication have been a big part of my life despite experiencing painful shyness. I fight shyness to this day. One-on-one conversations are much harder for me than speaking across the distance between me and an audience.

After a few attempts at storytelling and poetry recitation that resulted in the panic of shyness and frozen throat during elementary school, I found my niche in speech class and debate in junior high.

I had a very successful high school and university debating career. I won multiple University Scholastic League Awards all four years in high school and won a couple of tournaments that included a college scholarship as part of the prize. In college, we won some tournaments and the team placed 9th in the Phi Kappa Delta National Tournament one year.

That was a huge success for a university with about 10,000 students. We had a small eight member team. We competed against dozens of schools, including Ivy League schools like Harvard and large universities like UCLA.

All of the speaking skills I developed helped my communication through writing, too. However, I saw them as disconnected things, not compatible or con-joined. After all, they were always separate classes and activities in high school and college. Thus, they were fragmented in my mind.

So, I launched a verbal protest when a college professor lowered my grade on a paper stating that if I could be on the university debating squad, I could do better writing. My argument was that writing and speaking weren't the same any more than writing and using a shovel were, but I still got that "B." Now, I agree with him. Sometimes I actually speak out loud what I am writing to be sure the rhythm is right. It's all vibration and it's either in tune with the Universe or it's not.

Much later in life, I realized the sheer power of vibration while attending a sound healing conference in Santa Fe, New Mexico. In one of the classes we recreated what must be the way the Universe experiences expansion. A cluster of people chanted, while we stood in concentric circles around them. As their chanting built up the energy in the room, the circles of people around them began to be pushed back. We couldn't resist the power of that vibration and had to step back and expand our circles. After we were forced back several times, I realized that we had recreated the expansion of the Universe! It was eye opening and the reason I sometimes read my writing out loud to see if it is in tune with the subject matter. I want it to be expansive. I didn't know this as a student, however.

Debate was probably Spirit's way of helping me keep my voice alive. I grew up in an environment where I was not encouraged to use my voice. I was punished for speaking up and trying to set boundaries, even with the creepy uncle who violated the most sacred of boundaries. I would be forced to acquiesce to him if I tried to tell him to stay away from me. If I spoke up for myself against other family members, I was the problem for pointing out I never was the problem. No one wanted to deal with a bully or bother to protect me. I had no sanctity. I was on my own. However, the Universe did it's best to keep my vocal and communication energy active. For that I am grateful.

Debating for over nine years served me well. I developed a lot of confidence while speaking publicly. I became a volunteer trainer for the Mid-West Center for Nonprofit Leadership at UMKC. I was co-chair of a Greater Kansas City coalition Education Committee that helped bring more awareness to the law enforcement and judicial community about the effects of domestic violence on children. I was a paid executive trainer for a national childcare company. I also did a lot of training for the Early Childhood teachers who worked for me over the years. While it wasn't technically a training gig, that's what I did later at the newspaper too. We taught people about their communities and what was happening.

I had spent so many hours researching in libraries and law libraries on debating and extemporaneous speech topics, I could research an issue and pull it together for publication in the newspaper at the speed of light.

It also taught me to look someone (usually the only judge in the room) right in the eyes when communicating information and ideas. Looking that judge in the eyes also taught me to read body language, "Am I making my point? Is he/she bored? Should I speak faster or slower?" It helped some with my shyness.

In Extemporaneous Speech competition, you had a couple of hours to pull together research and ten minutes to make a convincing argument. You had to think, act and speak on your feet. It all served me well over the years.

Being the Co-Editor of my high school newspaper had helped me communicate through writing. I wrote what I thought was a filler article about how the god of Janus related to our senior year in high school. Our school sponsor saw it and demanded to know who wrote it. I replied I had written it in case we needed something to fill in. She firmly replied, "Oh no. This goes on the front page!"

I even pulled a one hundred for my story, "The Mystery of the Yellow Feather." from the most demanding English teacher *ever*, but yet I didn't see writing as viable for me or connected to talking. I just didn't pull the edges of communication together into one bundle for most of my life. I was the frazzle. I saw a bit of dazzle here and there, but never understood the cosmic vibration behind it all.

I'm not sure why I held the belief that I couldn't write regardless of that article or that one hundred, but I'm certain it was planted in my brain by very demanding parents. One incident probably carried more weight than it should have, but I suspect it created a negative trigger. Shaming can have lasting effects.

I came home from kindergarten and proudly proclaimed I could write in cursive. My father demanded proof of my newly claimed skill. Like any other five-year-old, I made a series of loops across the paper. My dad who was big on finding and punishing every mistake you might make, proclaimed me a liar. He informed me that what I was doing wasn't cursive writing. He berated me for claiming I could do something I couldn't do. I was lying. I was scribbling. Liars were punished.

Dad made me practice writing my name in cursive over and over because, "I had lied to him." It took weeks of exhaustedly practicing something my young motor skills weren't equipped to handle. My psyche was damaged by the oppressive punishment.

Finally, I was able to write my name in cursive to his satisfaction. Then, just as I thought that was all over and that I had learned my lesson successfully, I made another mistake.

I got into trouble in kindergarten class because I started putting my name on my papers in cursive trying to satisfy Dad. The teacher made me stop writing my name in cursive. I was to go back to printing my name. I was in a dilemma and scared to write my name at all. It seems I couldn't make anyone happy with my writing.

I think I maintained that limiting thought, regardless of my successes in school or life. No one would ever be happy with what/how I was writing. I doubt it will surprise my readers to know that I never received high marks for penmanship as I progressed through school.

Regardless of how I felt about writing, though. Spirit kept asking, "Can you hear me now? You need to be writing." Unfortunately, I couldn't quite accept the message regardless of what I did or was told.

Through the years of volunteering to create school, church and organizational newsletters, I heard more than once, "You've missed your calling. You should be writing." I would shrug or shake my head. I didn't think I was writing-not really. I have no idea what I thought "real" writing was, I just didn't think I was doing it. I sure didn't want to hear anyone say I wasn't writing correctly as had my dad and teacher. I was certain my writing wouldn't make anyone happy or that they might *want* to read what I wrote. I had learned everything I needed to know in kindergarten. I was a fraud.

Much later, I worked for several years in the domestic violence field. We were required to submit stories to the board about the families in our program. I became known for my ability put the emotions of having to seek shelter and a new life down on paper and make the board members cry with my written words. I still didn't put two and two together.

VI

Life moved forward. Decades later, I abruptly moved back home to help my aging parents. I was to find out just how bad things were at home after I took that giant leap of faith. First I received a very strong message that there was an ongoing, unacknowledged, and worsening health crisis and family situation. It also had implications for my writing.

That fateful day, I had gone to a hardware store for some things for my lawnmower. Going home, I received a literal blast of energy from the heavens. I pulled off the highway and burst into tears from the enormity of the energy. I heard no words, but words are just vibration. I received the information loud and clear.

I picked up my phone and placed the call. To my, and my parents' shock, I said, "I'm coming home." I never told them why. They were proud. I just didn't leave. I allowed them to think whatever they wanted to think about the situation. I knew if I told them why I was coming back, their pride of being in their 80s and 90s and independent would get in the way of what God wanted me to do. So, I stuck in there like a burr in a dog's coat helping them and protecting them as best as I could.

I joined a psychic development group in the nearby big city to meet new people. There, again, I kept hearing messages that I was supposed to be writing. As a funny side note, I was kicked out of the group because, "I wasn't trying hard enough to learn to be psychic." While I was mulling over that shocking turn of events, other group members let me know they had been kicked out too for similar reasons. It's funny sometimes how Spirit moves you along to better places and people.

I wasn't having any success finding a new job after my race home. Despite a lot of experience, licenses, and credentials, I was unemployed for months.

Finally listening to all the messages, I thought, "What the heck? I'll give writing a try." I began writing and submitting articles that were published online. I even completed a one hundred articles in one hundred days challenge. To my shock, thousands of people began reading my articles.

I'm certain Spirit was snickering the whole time. Go ahead and laugh, too. Not long after completing that one hundred articles in one hundred days challenge, I received my only job offer. I spent the next nine plus years becoming a multi-award-winning journalist, despite the attempt to have me fired for writing about those rocks.

Later I realized that Chiron considered a minor planet and The Wounded Healer had entered Pisces in February of that same year and right before my interview. Pisces is the sign for imaginative writers. Well, guess what? My Rising Sign is Pisces.

While I leaned much more in direction of a Piscean description than I did my Sun Sign of Virgo, each sign is good in its own way for feature writing or news reporting. I was blessed to do both in my position with the newspaper.

I, then, improved my photography by taking many photos of events I was covering. Subsequently, my art benefitted as my photography improved. I began to use photography for storytelling. Yes, more ways of communication.

If only I had known about astrology sooner, my life might have made sense earlier. God was probably standing arms akimbo and tapping his toe just waiting for me to pull it all together. I would like to think I would have embraced my true self more if I had known, but it could be that I needed this hindsight and that crooked path I wandered along.  My frazzle was working toward being dazzling.

Mercury, a planet named for the Messenger of the Gods, left footprints all over the day I was born that communication would be a dominant factor in this life. First of all, he was a messenger. Now I look back and want to yell, "Helllooooo. Lillie, where were you?" Just remember I had no exposure to any of this knowledge until later in life. While I certainly exhibited the influences of the planets, I didn't know how to take advantage of them even after I knew about such things.

While writing this book, I realized I had unknowingly gotten a tattoo that was representative of Mercury some twenty years ago. I have a caduceus tattoo on my back. Mercury has been evident in my life in many ways.

The planet Mercury is positioned in my Seventh House. It's a bit crowded in that house with some other stuff, but it's all related. That house is about partnerships. While it might mean marriage or business partners, I have come to believe it is about a partnership with Spirit and allowing Spirit to speak through me in a variety of ways.

The Seventh House is also about the love of a good debate. Hmmm where have I heard the word debate before? My Mercury is in conjunction with my sun sign of Virgo meaning I have a strong drive for communication. It's sextile with Mars where that word debate comes up again. It's trine with Lilith where proactive speech comes into play again. Lilith also helps a person see the flaws of a situation.

That certainly came in handy in competitive debating, along with investigating and covering local politics for the newspaper. My ability to read body language and psychic hits helped too. It wasn't unusual to hear, "How did you know that?"

My Pluto is in the Sixth House. That's not surprising as I was always asking questions, and looking for open ended answers that left me with more and deeper thought questions. A neighbor who was teaching me to create a stained-glass panel looked at me in aggravation and said, "You ask the damned-ist questions I ever heard!"

Pluto in the 6th House means I couldn't rest until I researched every aspect of a topic, but that didn't always serve me well. There are times you just need to trust or be okay with where you are. Unfortunately, I felt incomplete or unacceptable if I didn't know *everything* about something. That has been a challenge in my spiritual growth. Spirit needs to be accepted, more than understood. For school, debating, and work, it was a blessing.

So, there is all is, laid out in my astrology chart. Can you believe it? The planets actually line up in the heavens to bring it all together!

If only I had known.

That's why telling your story is important, though. You can save others a lot of steps and anguish and see yourself in a different light. What seems to be frazzle is actually points of light that dazzle!

While I was busy hacking my way through the underbrush trying to find my true path, it was, as so many movies told me, inside me all along. It wasn't about location, location, location. It was about communication, communication, communication! Well, I guess it was about location too, though. The location of those planets.

However, in addition to the planetary alignments there were those numbers in my birthday. There is a sequence of 91919. That alone is significant, but the number one relates to innovation, creativity, thinking out of the box and upgrading to new levels of being. Nines relate to eternity, faith, working with light, expansive viewpoints, intuition, synchronicities and, surprise, communication. It also represents the connecting with others on a spiritual level. They add up to the spiritual mastery number of 11. I see the numbers 919 frequently. In fact, I am seeing the numbers 119 at 9:09 right now while I'm writing this portion of my story. Number synchronicities show up frequently..

Chiron, the Wounded Healer showed up for more than just healing the implanted idea that writing could be emotionally challenging. When I arrived back home, things were much worse than I thought; not only my mother's health, but the emotional situation my parents were in at the hands of a selfish and abusive family member mentioned before. I wouldn't find out just how bad until after they both had passed away.

As I mentioned, it took that spiritual trumpet blast to pull me to the side of the road that day. That's what it took to make me wipe out my, as I knew it, and begin again in a new way--Spirit's way. Yet, I didn't go down easy. As you read, I still wasn't accepting all the messages I was hearing.

Even on the day I was packing to move, Spirit kept leaving me messages that it was the right decision. I kept finding three to five dimes by my bed. I would pick them up and put them on the bed. Later more dimes would be on the floor. In the twentieth century dimes were imprinted with the portrait of Mercury. Hmmmm there's that messenger again.

Moving was an easy decision to make, but a very hard one to execute. I was satisfied with my life. I had friends and a social life. I enjoyed my healing work. I suppose Spirit had been calling and knocking, getting louder and louder, but that day it was clear. Obviously, Spirit had a plan and was determined to fulfill it, or at least part of it. Otherwise, what unfolded wouldn't have happened.

I learned the newspaper business from bottom to top and reported on just about everything under the sun. I really enjoyed writing and the creativity of it all. I won several Texas Press Association Awards, a Freedom of Speech Award and a couple of Appreciation Awards from the school district and other organizations I helped. I was pretty content over the next nearly decade. I loved the variety of topics, photography and never dull moments in area politics. Let's not forget, I thought I was finally doing what the Great Spirit wanted me to do. I was writing nearly every day.

VII

Then, without expecting it, I was back in a similar challenging spot, but now a decade later. This time I recognized my life had been wiped clean for a fresh start and for different reasons. I wasn't really sure why the writing position was removed from me. I had no idea what was in store.

It became pretty apparent I had been running on adrenaline and stress. I had no idea how hard I had been running and how out of spiritual and physical breath I was until I tried to stop.

My position as journalist had me working at least five days a week and many nights and weekends a month. I was also helping my parents in their last days while my brother made everyone's life miserable every chance he had, especially our parents whenever I wasn't home. I was often up all night in the ER with one of them and struggling to stay awake the next day at work. My brother was "too busy" to take an overnight turn in the hospital although, he didn't have job to get up and go to the next day. In less than three years of each other, my parents passed away-both of them ill, bullied and stressed, but having led long lives.

Those ugly family situations that seem like they only exist in bad novels or movies? Well, sometimes they are real and this one was. I eventually realized the bad home situation had been developing for many, many years, probably all of my life. I knew I had to deal with being bullied, but looking back, it wasn't just me. That was a big part of the reason Spirit yelled through that energetic megaphone, "Go home!"

After Mom's funeral, family members told me about the abuse they had witnessed over the years. I wasn't surprised because I came home one day to see marks on Mom's face that she wouldn't discuss. It may have been nothing, but I had worked in the field of domestic violence long enough to be suspicious when things didn't seem right.

I witnessed my brother storm into their house and berate our parents over simple things like forgetting how to reprogram the cable remote at age 90. He yelled at them frequently for spending their own money, because they were, "Spending his inheritance." He bullied them over spending money to go see their grandchildren, even for weddings, and had to be paid to help them with anything, including going to the doctor.

I had to perform energy clearings on the house nearly everyday. I used protection around where mom and dad sat and I called daily on the angels to help keep us safe.

Community members and family members told me about the lies my brother had been spreading about me. Some of them were so ridiculous I had to shake my head over anyone believing them. One of the most ridiculous things he did was to follow me around the town where I worked. The town has less than 5000 people and is only about 4 square miles. How hard to you think it was to know I was being followed? I have no idea what his purpose was, but stalking is another form of bullying. Perhaps intimidation was his only purpose.

My uncle told me about hearing the lies and knowing they were lies. He visited and talked with Dad often while Dad was dying. He told me how my brother had demanded thousands of dollars of me and demanded that dad force me to pay him. Later he tried to force mom to demand income tax returns from me. My uncle told me he witnessed what he considered neglect of his only living brother, at the hands of his son. My aunt told me, that years before, she had witnessed dad being physically assaulted. It explained some things I had questioned all of my life and actually, it wasn't surprising.

My brother had burst into my room one day and started choking me. He frequently hurled objects at me for no reason. He stole things from me and said what he could to make mom and dad upset with me. He did so many petty things like blocking my car in the garage to make me late for school, that I lost count. Unfortunately, he never outgrew such behaviors.

It makes me sad, but yet it could be that the karma of my parents being abusive themselves played a role in how he treated them. I'm not going to judge that though. Having experienced it myself, I can tell you no one deserves to be abused, whether it be emotional, mental, or physical. Sadly, the three of us experienced it all.

Unfortunately, the family bully wasn't done just yet. I ended up suddenly homeless by his hands within days of Mom's death. I wasn't really surprised. All of my childhood, he had taken things from me that I had worked for and even taken things from my home decades later. My things regularly disappeared after I moved back home. I might arrive home from work only to face parental anger over some lie they had been told. One ironic day, they were told that I had never gone to work. They demanded to know what I was doing instead of working. What? It was mind bobbling. It was a vicious, abusive wheel of violence fuelded by the family bully.

Strong, loyal family and friends and a heaping dose of Spiritual intervention got me through that terrible time. I was provided a supportive place to stay and surrounded with caring people.

Two months later, I was emotionally slammed again. The owner of the newspaper retired and closed up the business giving me a one-day notice and no severance pay. My life had done received another wham, bam, but it sure didn't hear, "Thank you ma'am," from me.

Now I had plenty of time to rest and study, but the noise of anxiety and grief was deafening. When I felt like I was drowning a bit less and with firm support from a friend, I knuckled down even more on spiritual/self-studies, and tried to pull myself together.

I continued the part time intuitive reading and healing work I had started a couple of years before. Unfortunately, the work environment at the metaphysical center was less than ideal and I decided to walk away with nowhere else to turn. However, I had learned that when it doesn't work out, there is often a spiritual reason.

At least I had stood up for myself instead of letting my voice be silenced there too. It was back to resting and learning. Frankly, I needed a lot more of that selfcare. I wasn't ready and Spirit knew it.

I also started back on a lifelong pursuit, again, with the firm support of the friend who offered me shelter. I had always wanted to be an artist. My grandmother had introduced me to painting when I was little, but my parents didn't support that idea, or many of the ideas I had. Their imaginations were much less expanded than the one God gave to me. I was never allowed to take lessons or take art class in high school. The desire never left me though. In adulthood I struggled to learn to paint on my own.

I needed to release that childhood implant that I had to be perfect if I wanted a crumb or two of love or acceptance. Spirit, though, wanted me to learn that painting or any other activity didn't need to be work. Why the work reference?

I was required to work as a child and not just chores. I needed to find a job on every day off from school, except Sunday. I was even rousted from my sick bed the second day the doctor sent me to bed. I had contracted the mumps in the Spring of my Senior year of high school. My dad declared me lazy and forced me from bed to clean the house, do laundry and cook dinner. The mumps spread in what was called "going down on you." I missed almost three weeks of school. My grades never recovered and I missed being an Honor Student for graduation by a fraction of a point. I was the only Senior member of the National Honor Society unable to stand on stage that night. Luckily, the mumps didn't reach my reproductive organs or I might not have had children.

I was well programmed to work and not take care myself. I had to make an activity look like work, or I couldn't do it. I eventually began to call myself the family slave. It was what it was.

Trying to turn everything into a job, so it wouldn't seem frivolous and taken away from me didn't show up just when I was painting. Eventually that's how I came to realize why I did many of the things I did and why I had such a hard time resting or relaxing. I even tried to overachieve in relationships.

I don't sleep well either. Some of that was fear of the dark, some of it was the things that go bump in the night and some of it was because people came into my room when I was sleeping. Those things left strong implants in my psyche.

I came to understand I was in constant flight or fight mode and that's why I struggled to slow down and take care of myself. It was like my nervous system had gone into defibrillation, short cycling, always poised for danger. I was mentally, emotionally, physically, and sometimes spiritually exhausted.

Before the exhaustion realization happened and all that much deeper work began, my mother passed away, the last of my parents. I think she and Dad both just gave up. A dear friend of theirs told me mom had said she was sick of my brother coming over every day ranting and raving about me when I was just going to work and helping them. Dad had told my Uncle he was glad I was there with them, but apparently not everyone was happy. After dad was gone, mom was the lone victim and I'm sure that was much harder for her. There was no one to protect her during the day.

Between Mom's death, my brother finding a way to evict me from the home I was supposed to inherit, then suing me over leaving the house keys in the garage, and my job ending, I had a lot to process, even months later. More information about what had happened during my parents' lives just kept coming, but Spirit was helping me cope.

VIII

On the night of the anniversary of Mom's death and feeling sad, I felt an urge to write. Suddenly poetry poured through my fingers as they typed. Poetry? "Well," I thought, "It's still a form of my life-long connection to communication." The poetry flowed quickly and easily, much like my experience with a Butterfly Haiku in college.

As the rhythm of the words easily appeared on the paper that anniversary night, I knew the message was divinely guided. As those words flowed, raw and real, feelings suddenly shifted. I knew that was the purpose of the poem.

By then I had experienced all kinds of things. Living with my parents was no different. I saw Dad in the house several times after he passed and Mom saw him too.

A few hours after she passed, Mom turned off the lamp in my bedroom. It kind of buzzed as it went off and back on again. After a few seconds, I realize it must be her. I asked if she was alright and she turned the light off again as an answer. She has played with the lights a few times since. One just recently that left me a bit freaked out.

The home I am living in is large and u-shaped. I had left the light on in the bathroom as I was going to finish the last few minutes of a television show I was watching on the other side of the house. I turned off all the lights expecting that one light to guide me to the back of the house.

Blinded by turning off the lights at the end of the show, I crept along through the house. I realized there was no light on. I turned the corner and thought to myself, "I thought I left that light on?"

As soon as I thought that, the light buzzed, looked a little weird and turned on. I froze. Now logically I knew there was no one in the house. The security on the doors dings when they are opened, but there is a door right across from the bathroom door.

Scenes from scary movies flashed through my head. I had to walk past the bathroom to my room. Was Jason and his ax in there? Was some ghost going to grab me? It was silly, but the dark can still get to me. I knew it was likely Mom. She typically comes during storms and turns off a light like she did the night she died. It was raining.

I sucked in some Spiritual strength, checked out the bathroom anyway and turned out the light. I tried to turn it on again, but it wouldn't turn on the first two times I tried it. I thought to myself, "Very funny, Mom." It finally turned on. I hunkered down in my bed, though, and pulled up the covers just for good measure

WHEN GRIEF BECAME JUST A WORD

By Lillie Ruby January 22, 2021

The grueling of grieving that filled my days,
On one final day it seemed swept away.
Now a memory and you know who you are,
Some of you near, others so far.
Tears and I are nearly spent.
Overnight, the tears just went.
Surprised, I realized something had shifted.
Thankfully, my head and heart were lifted.
It was hump day in so many ways.
Yes, that Wednesday was a fateful day.
There was nothing new that I had done.
I just realized that the pain had not won.
Instead of being an all-consuming verb.
Grief had become just a word.

IX

While experiences like that were interesting and mostly comforting, they weren't as common to me as other things. By the time my parents passed over to the other side, I had been a channel for decades. I imagine I always have been. My first memory of channeling came at about age eleven. Don't let that Master Spiritual number of eleven escape you. Not that I am a Spiritual Master, but I had masterful spiritual help that day.

At that time, I had no name or recognition of what I was doing. What I was doing would have probably been denounced on Sunday if anyone had known I could be considered a Channel, much less that I now actively pursue that calling.

That has always seemed strange to me. Call it what you will. Why was listening to spiritual messages, conveying them or perhaps writing them down an issue? Even the Bible says that God speaks to us. I have never, and never will understand why a name or description matters or determines what's right or wrong. I have simply listened and sometimes served as God/Spirit's Oracle. I've not been running around as hell's minion. I digress. So, back to my first memory of channeling.

I clearly remember that day because no one in my family listened much to what I had to say. This time my parents actually listened, so it is time-stamped in my memory.

My brother had a carbuncle on his knee. If you don't know

what that is, basically, it is a super boil. For several days my parents had been giving first aid treatment to it without much success.

I watched my brother's overly dramatic response to their work while eating my breakfast. Long story short, I walked over and told them precisely what needed to happen. As I said, surprisingly, they listened. They had me repeat it and demonstrate what I was saying. I'm sure Spirit intervened with them so the message could be heard, regardless of the source.

There was more drama from my brother. Much to his irritation at having to follow his younger sister's instructions, it worked! In a few days the infection was healed.

I was about 10-11 years old. At that age, I had no way of knowing any medical information. I just "knew what to do." It was accurate information because it came from Spirit and I was the conduit, or Oracle. It is my first memory of channeling.

Channeling occurred at other times, but again, I really had no reference point. It's just that sometimes it stuck in my memory like knowing how to treat a carbuncle.

I sometimes blurted out things in blunt, but truthful ways and then stood in shock at what had come tumbling out of my mouth. Other times I left the same shocked expression on faces at what profound words (Not mine) I had just uttered. One friend told me in frustration, "When you say stuff like that, I have to go home and think for hours about what you said." I reiterated, "That's because they aren't *my* words. It's a message."

While I worked at the domestic violence shelter, the Director had commented to one of the therapists, "I don't know how to deal with all of the profound things that came out of Lillie's mouth." It was a pretty common experience to see those stunned faces, or to answer the phone at work and be told something I had written had, "Hit me in the heart."

I was well aware I wasn't thinking up that stuff. I would simply wait to see what came out. I just hoped I didn't need a cleanup on aisle one if the information was delivered too bluntly. I didn't want to hurt anyone, but sometimes I didn't have control, God did.

I still laugh when I think about the wary look, I received from a guy I had been seeing. He asked me a question that I thought required some consideration before I replied. As I sat there, he said, "Don't be afraid to tell me what you think." I looked at him in surprise and said, "I'm not afraid to answer you. I'm waiting to see what I think." After his wary look, I realized how odd that sounded. I was waiting to see what God and I thought. That seems like a good plan to me.

As I considered what happened that night, I began to realize just how often I stopped and waited for Spirit to answer something for me, or give me advice. I rarely heard words, but I would cock my head to the right to listen to the vibration and convey that into words. I was channeling as a regular practice, rather than only as a formal sit-down practice. I just hadn't realized it, as it was an integral part of my life.

Spirit has a lot to say and will deliver the message anyway possible. Clearly, it sometimes used me. Don't forget, along this crooked way, I realized that the astrological Seventh House of partnership was about me partnering with Spirit to communicate. Without realizing it though, I was still resisting some of it even while actively participating in spiritual communication.

During my stint at the newspaper, I also channeled several editorials that were honored by the press association. I would hear the word editorial loudly in my right ear and sit down at the keyboard. The topic would decided by Spirit and the words would flow. I also used keyboard automatic writing to tap into spiritual guidance at home most days. Sometimes I wrote by hand, but not very often. I usually couldn't read what I had written with my less than perfect handwriting.

By now, I knew what it was and that I was channeling and auto writing spiritual information. I also realized I was processing spiritual vibration through my psychic ears into guidance. Guidance people got whether either of us expected it or not.

It took many years to realize that's what I had been doing. Only now, do I recognize it through some earlier events that happened. For example, the Butterfly Haiku I mentioned before.

Other than that poem on Mom's death anniversary, I didn't think I had ever written poetry. Now that I look back on it, thanks to this life review, I had at least one previous event of channeling spiritual poetry during a test in college English.

We had spent one day discussing Haiku poetry. Since it was only one day, it didn't seem to have much significance. I didn't pay enough attention and was unprepared to write a Haiku to answer a test question the next week.

I struggled for a while and finally just thought, "Screw it." I put down whatever came to my head about a butterfly. The professor gave me an extra ten points for that poem!

It is unfortunate that I never realized that extra ten points was a thumbs up from God. It was one of many signs that I could write, I just didn't pick up on the signs.

Now I realize, I let go and I channeled the poem. So, on the anniversary of mom's death, I was only surprised in that, after decades of being absent, more poetry showed up, not that I was channeling.

I have remembered while writing this life review, that I had channeled a sort of free-flowing type of poetry one day while walking the Prairie Labyrinth. The owner of the labyrinth had provided a brief class and measured our energy fields with dowsing rods before entering the labyrinth. She also provided paper copies of a seven-circuit labyrinth and a pen to use to record whatever came up while we walked the paths.

As soon as I stepped onto the first segment, I was overwhelmed with the urge to write. As I wrote around and around that paper labyrinth following the circuits, I couldn't stop. I was just re-cording the words I was receiving. There was no thought. Words flowed and filled up that paper labyrinth. Afterwards, I read some profound words from Spirit.

I wish I could include them here, but the paper labyrinth was packed away when I had to abruptly move. When it's time, they will resurface. In the meantime, I have learned that should I find myself stuck while writing, writing in circles can be very benefi-cial to breaking free from my mind-based dictator, Chatty Cathy.

X

Ok, so poetry was relatively new to me or at least little used, but now what? "Helllooooo, anybody out there?" I still couldn't slow down or find my path. I was frazzling more by the hour, by the day, or so I thought. I was looking everywhere I could think of looking, not realizing the truth of who I was becoming was all around me.

A couple of months later, my painting changed and for the better. I realized I had still been trying for perfection, approval and that ever elusive love crumb as a reward for working and not playing, or heaven forbid, enjoying myself. All day I cried my way through a painting and most of the next day, releasing pain and anger.

I was painting a rather large canvas and filling it with hydrangeas in spiritual colors. Not for that purpose, but because purples and blues have always been soothing colors for me.

At one point my mom got so tired of hearing that I wanted a purple room, she over reacted in just the perfect way. I loved my purple kingdom. The walls and shelves were purple. All the doors were purple. She dyed the bedspreads and even the rugs purple. There was purple everywhere. If heaven came in your favorite color, I had just entered the pearly gates.

I eventually looked up the meaning for hydrangea after painting that cluster of them. I discovered it means water barrel. As water and emotions are so closely tied, it was no wonder I felt the urge to paint hydrangeas while crying and shifting my emotions. After I completed that painting another poem emerged from my fingers.

Ok, so now I'm a better artist, and apparently my Higher Self has decided to dabble in poetry, but now what?

Then one day an intuitive message came to me. Painting was communication too. I was writing again, but differently.

By working through my inner conditioned restrictions and expectations, I had learned to channel Spirit through my heart and the vibration of words and color. Well, actually I was told that in a spiritual message, "Interpret light through the vibration of love with words and color."

While I briefly wondered about that message, I realized that was what had shifted. I channeled the vibration of spiritual love into that painting. When I do that, instead of falling off the wagon and making it a job, there is a big difference in how people react to the painting, even if it isn't technically correct.

I was beginning to have a lot of bits and pieces of a puzzle and, believe it or not, even participated in a global project to join paintings together as a puzzle. I still wondered, though, if everything in my life was destined to come in puzzle form and in indecipherable pieces that I must endlessly turn around and around hoping for a fit. I needed the box to see the big picture, please. I wanted to see "my path." I was feeling more and more frazzled. No matter what I experienced or learned, I was still stuck in that ideology of figuring out, knowing, and/or seeing one path. Although Spirit was continually speaking into my ears, it was often muffled. I was still stuck mentally, but I was progressing anyway. God can be wonderfully sneaky about helping us despite our fears.

Below is the first painting the author created letting another painting show through as background. By allowing the old painting to show, the artist shows transformation.

PAINTING AWAY PAIN

By Lillie Ruby April 19, 2020

Grief shows up when you least expect,
Leaving you wondering, "What the heck?"
A pretty day and feeling productive,
Painting away, happy and contructive.
Then, wham, bam, no thank you ma'am.
Tears now flowing. What is this sham?
I was feeling, oh so fine.
Everything was so pretty and aligned.
What is this that has erupted again?
When, oh when will I ever mend?
Grief you are a sneaky one.
Now I'm back, nearly where I begun.

XI

Well, as you can guess, that all-telling box didn't come in the mail. Nothing in particular, at least that I recognized as one path, came together either. I thought of this and that and other possibilities, but I was still scrambling around on the floor for that missing piece of the puzzle. I was still trying to question Spirit's plan and timeline, "Where was the big picture?"

Yes, I was tired, so tired of trying to figure it all out. "Why couldn't my path just appear?" I wondered. I wasn't feeling the dazzle, just the frazzle.

I often lamented to myself and other friends of the same ilk, "Why am I learning all of this if I'm to do nothing with it?" I kept receiving messages that said, "Wait. It's not time yet." I virtually banged my head on the table.

Even though I was learning that letting go was the key to so much, I was still often using my old mind that needed to find love through all the wrong actions: perfectionism, overworking, over-giving and always on alert to remain physically, emotionally, mentally and spiritually safe. I was quite the ninja, but you won't find that on my resume. I've learned (for the most part) if it isn't my circus, there is no reason to stand in the center ring trying to be the ball juggler. *That* spotlight light is simply blinding.

The thing is, I still felt like I had all those balls in the air without a place for them to land. I wondered, "What was I supposed to do?" I channeled message after message that I would be writing again, "When?" I asked. "It's not time yet," I heard. When?" I asked. "It's not time yet," I heard. "What should I write about?" I asked. "It's not time yet," I heard. The same answer was given about painting, writing poetry, and expanding intuitive skills.

I seemed to be in spiritually provided neutral. I was enjoying my creative time, but getting no closer to finding the missing piece of my life puzzle. There still seemed a thousand roads to travel to somewhere, but I still didn't know my destination or have a map. I kept falling back into old habits where trusting my intuition had less value than "work ethic." It was deep, deep conditioning and it was holding me back.

Eventually, my frustration with regularly hearing that it wasn't time for the great unveiling mushroomed into another poem after a meditation on timing.

I thought I finally understood the time reference, but somehow, I just couldn't quite leave it behind. I still wandered and wondered about a true path for me. I wasn't waiting patiently, despite all of the messages to wait, relax, rest. I was trying for something earthly instead of simply trusting. I was programmed for goals, expectations and a business plan. I felt more frazzled by the day and didn't feel the dazzle one bit.

In addition to that time related frustration, there was a steady supply of people telling me my throat chakra was blocked, out of balance and whatever else. My frustration grew and grew. How could my throat chakra have issues when my entire life had been about communication? So, I worked often to "clear out the gunk," and, at times, found some energetic cords that with Archangel Michael's help were removed. I was clearing that vessel, yet, the messages kept coming. That noise people were hearing was me banging my head. It was frustrating to say the least.

BEHIND THE FACE OF ALL THAT ISN'T

By Lillie Ruby 6/29/2020

I head the ticking, it went on and on.

Then in an instant, I was gone.

Where I went, I still don't know.

But behind the face it was quite a show.

There was everything I really didn't ken.

Bells, whistles, even coils and springs.

There was a whisper, Just let it BE.

You expect ME to sit under a Bodhi tree?

Like the White Rabbit giant clock in hand,

I went into a land where increments were banned.

Everything was moving, but going nowhere.

Much like me with confusing stare.

How can it be that nothing is something?

How can it be that something is nothing?

I covered my ears from the clicking and ding.

In my head I heard the big aha ring.

Wisdom from inside an imagined tick-tock.

Time is the KEY

AND

Time is the LOCK.

XII

A new twist for my communication skills and another head scratcher about my throat chakra showed up. I started channeling some sort of language I couldn't understand and even that was changing over time. Then, I finally realized that I had been using telepathic skills through my throat for a number of years. It was often an unpleasant experience that could leave me choking, coughing, clearing my throat and feeling a burning sensation.

I always thought telepathy was a brain activity. I was learning (I'll admit slowly) the obvious. My throat chakra was part of the grand communication plan for me and in ways I couldn't imagine. I was *so* confused at all of the developments, but probably because I was unknowingly resisting. To me, it seemed to be more frazzling.

I have come to believe since, that my throat also provides healing light energy while it is processing someone's harsh conversations or comments. It can be very unpleasant, but if it provides some good in this world, then I am grateful for its healing magic.

 In addition to the new activities being processed through my throat, I was also getting downloads that, to me and other people who could see them, looked like those numbers in the Matrix movie. Some days, there were golden glowing numbers streaming down from above me and entering the top of my head.

You see what pattern was forming? Yeah, neither did I. Stuff was happening, but for what end result? I had no idea. Where was my path? It was all frazzle to me.

A few months before these new things began to appear, a spiritual message came for me that I needed to expand my consciousness. I thought I had been. I'm sure I was. The message, however, had me thinking that I was probably trying to put normal, dogma type parameters around the process because that's pretty much what my Spiritual Guides said. The difference this time was that Spirit told me what to do (sort of). As you've read, I heard "Let the frazzle be your dazzle."

First, though, I was to continue to review what comprised my frazzle. There was a lot to review, but it was mainly about resistance to how I expected my life to look, compared to how it was actually unfolding.

XIII

"A jack of all trades is a master of none, but oftentimes better than a master of one," is what I finally figured out my guides were going for (after some nudging) with, "Let Your Frazzle Be Your Dazzle." Their statement certainly was a bit more interesting than that old phrase, but I wanted to learn more. A little digging put more light onto the old phrase (pun intended).

A jack, at least as far back as the 14th century, connotated a small piece of the greater whole whether it be a person or thing. The term was later adapted for ships as a jack flag to alert the Harbor Master to the various purposes a ship served. A jack flag could also serve to show a ship's country of origin. The jack flag could show that a ship was carrying camels, clothing or wine etc. Basically, the jack flag became a form of communication designating cargo within the ship or fleet, and for communication with the Harbor Master.

An application of the term jack could apply in more modern times in this way. Your home may have a jack in the wall for your internet modem. That device serves to create a connection to a greater communication network, the telephone company and the internet. It is a small part of a greater whole that communicates with us, thus a jack.

Ok, now what I heard was beginning to make some sense. The frazzle is the jack and I (and You) am a stepped-up version of the jack that is part of the Universe, God, Greater Consciousness, (Whatever you want to call it), but the greater whole. Was that clear? No, not really, but I seemed to be getting it.

Why would my spiritual advisors even address this with me? I did the obvious and asked.

So many programs and ideology that sprang up over the past one hundred years, or so, and from just about everywhere: education, business, even metaphysics etc., have focused on finding your "one true path/career." That idea was pushed on children as soon as they could talk, "What do you want to be when you grow up?" The desire to be one thing, even from the mind of a four-year old was encouraged. Focusing on it for life was revered, as was one job your entire life until you got the clock at retirement. Life has been programmed to be based on asking, "What do you want to do?" There is little interest in knowing how you want to be in the world, or what you want to explore.

This approach is a dichotomy in a world where for hundreds of generations people needed to know how to do most everything themselves. They needed to be that jack of all trades. The men might be out hunting one week, and repairing saddles or roofs the next. Even the best sword in the land needed to know how to sew up a wound, or carve a cradle for the pending arrival of a new baby. Women were equally diverse in what they did. They were capable of being the local medicine healer, the cook, defending the home when the men weren't home, or the creators of fabric and fashion. Children were trained in how to do all of these things so that as adults they could survive and support their community. It was the way of life for thousands of years.

Then the tide shifted with the start of the industrial age and continued to be narrowed in focus. Culture moved from teaching children to survive by knowing as much as possible to a society where children are supposed to choose just one thing to be good at doing.

I don't know a single person who was ever asked how to they wanted to be in this world. (If you were, believe me, you are blessed.) Even play time became regimented and now children are encouraged to become world-class athletes at tender ages instead of learning to climb trees for strength, agility and perhaps to learn about the fruit, bark, and leaves for survival. We have made ourselves rather helpless without an expert or collective of experts somewhere to consult or do the work for us.

If a pipe breaks, we are without water until the plumber knocks on the door to fix the pipe. Instead of a general practitioner, we go to doctors who specialize in bits of our bodies instead of a wholistic approach. Even the elementary school teacher is supplemented by reading specialists, speech therapists etc. Attorneys specialize in criminal defense or real estate. Even law enforcement and professional sports teams have special teams. You see what I mean. We have become segmented in thought and action instead of functioning as a spiritually whole person and society.

As that limiting mind set developed, companies began to form and isolate tasks in the hope of creating speed, perfection and, of course, more profitability for the owners. Adults are now expected to be experts at something, even if it's sorting screws all day. Strangely enough, it's not good to be that jack of all trades and have sustainability. The entrepreneur can be seen as a threat.

A resurgence of the multi-talented individual occurred a few decades ago in cottage crafts and businesses. A lot of that was quickly turned into isolated bits and pieces, too. Big companies started competing and taking over that bit of independence in business and the entrepreneurial income, while keeping the isolated skill model in place. While the independent business is still alive, its spiritual potential was quickly swallowed.

Bit by bit, people began to see themselves as some bit of frazzle. If a person didn't have one major skill for a job, or one that they were perfecting, he/she had little expectation of success. The industrial design was the fragmenting of something designed by Spirit to be whole. It pretended to be a whole, but in reality, it was the fragmenting of skills for speed and monetary gain.

This model has nothing much to do with happiness. It really made little sense for the individual and mainly served industrial production. I can see where it created a lot of frazzle in the world and that carried over into my way of thinking and conditioning, too.

That was exactly where I trudged. I tried not to buy into the ideology, but underneath all the struggle I still did. I knew I wasn't a one size fits all, but I wanted to be, just so I would feel loved. It didn't work though. The more I frazzled, the more I was rejected. The more I was rejected, the more I was dejected.

I wasn't sure who I was, but I knew I wasn't being myself. I felt I had to dim my light around people to avoid the rejection. It didn't help much, though. I was still rejected and I just couldn't help allowing my inner self to peek through at times. I had no idea there was any dazzle in my life, I just knew it was work trying to be accepted.

The ideology of choosing what you wanted to be from infancy hasn't fit for many people, and I was one of those. I always loved bright, shiny and colorful things and finding ways to change up the furniture or even a flower bed. My mother told me she never had flowers in the yard because I always picked them to decorate the house (and probably hoping to make her happy with me). I loved other so-called frivolous things and activities. I was dazzled and jazzed by crystals and wind chimes. One of the few bright spots in college was taking geology classes. I was always imagining change and possible improvement to just about everything.

My dolls were always styling in fabric scraps my grandmother got from the local (and famous) formal dress factory. For fun, I sometimes wondered whose dress fabric I was working with, "Was it for Miss America, or some famous actress?" Many famous women wore creations from that factory back in the day, and I could have been using the scraps from one of their dresses.

I have created, changed and recreated all types of things all through my life. I've lived in over a dozen homes in several states, and I've changed things in and around every one of them. After all,

I needed to fit in my own home (skin).

I still laugh at a meditation I participated in. During that meditation, I traveled spiritually to a monk monastery. I was excited to see the building surrounded by sand Zen gardens and a rake standing nearby. As I gleefully picked up a rake and headed to change the design, a monk ran out waving his hands and telling me to get away. As I turned and asked why, he said, "Every time you come here you change up our work." Surprised, I had no idea I had been there before, but the monk clearly knew me. I argued some about being allowed to rake, but he held firm. He finally said, "Fine, there is a pile of sand back behind the building. You can rake there, but don't touch the garden." Well, I grumbled, but found the pile and an entire area to create my vision.

That's how am I, though. I am not ok with one thing, or often even one thing at a time. I need to be creating, something, whatever that may be. As a childhood friend once said to me, "It's like you are driven to create." I am. It's how God made me. The world to me has been an itchy wool sweater. I couldn't wait to get a sweater off and try on something else, or learn about something new. I am the square peg in a Swiss cheese world. Life is a buffet, but I've got a platter instead of a plate.

There can never be enough choices! All of those choices are exciting to me, not overwhelming. I just get frustrated with so little time in this life, and the uncertainly about how to pull it all together. I've dibbled and dabbled and had some fun, but not dazzled very much, at least in my eyes.

My parents, however, fit into that thinking mold of one job forever. A career was chosen for me if I wanted to go to college, so I dropped my head and trudged toward graduation. I wanted to learn and experience a bigger world than our small town, so I did what it took. I wanted to, "Get the heck out of Dodge."

Except for geology, there was no color or shiny in my classes, but I trudged on. Professors who knew me asked what I was thinking. They bluntly, but honestly, told me I wasn't meant for the career I had to choose. They were right. I hated being trapped in a systemic box. I wasn't created to be one of the people who thrive in that situation. As a result, I have avoided that line of work as much as possible unless I could maneuver myself into a position with a lot more freedom.

Honestly, it was a waste of the gifts God gave me. Looking back, it seems like someone was trying to erase my planet-ed chart. Maybe that was the case, or not, but my life played into the thinking of one person, one path.

It was frustrating. I kept seeing all these interesting trails going off into the woods. I was becoming more frazzled by the day because trying to stuff me in some bland, tan box simply didn't work.

What I have come to realize, is this type of thinking and pressure of choosing only one path is a way of controlling, and also creating a ceiling mentally and emotionally. Diversity of thinking, skills and creativity were a sure cause of rebellion, change, evolution and possible success.

My parents had seen that in me from the moment I was born. They did not celebrate a creative, independent, and free-spirited daughter. Those characteristics were discouraged, often physically, for their comfort. They weren't completely erased, though, even by the pain. The God-given drive in me was just too strong. The possibilities were too endless. Inside my skin, I was a big container of glitter waiting to explode.

One job I had might seem a bit out of synch for me if you knew what it was, but it brought me in contact with a man who actually owned the patents for a lot of the industrial psychological tests used commercially. Dr. Ed had worked for large companies and also founded and sold several of his own. At that time, he was primarily retired, but he applied his wares on, I must say, unsuspecting "test-ees." I had to take his tests for the job. I'm sure, now, that was a big part of the spiritual reasons I was steered into that job.

Dr. Ed gave the darndest tests I've ever taken, but one of them is the point of this story. I had no idea what any of the tests were for. By then, I was several tests into whatever the process was. I was just trying to make it through the testing without losing my new job. It turned out this particular test assessed your abilities to imagine, visualize, create, etc.

Dr. Ed came to the office to review my testing with me. He was already irritated with me because I was beating his IQ tests. I had no idea what the tests had been for, or that I was beating them and jumping my scores upward against all odds and statistics. I was just breathing and waiting for answers from above because those tests felt like a game of whack-a-mole with me the likely mole. Thankfully, he abandoned trying to box in my IQ after three tests with increasing scores.

That day, Dr. Ed unfolded a large 11x14 sheet of paper and asked if I saw the graphing he had done. "Yes," I replied. He then unfolded another large piece he had taped to the upper right corner, and showed me the graphing continued right to the edge of that second sheet of paper. He grumpily said, "I thought I was going to have to tape another piece of paper to this." I waited. He said, "You are the most creative person I have ever tested in over forty years of doing this." I laughed. As he peered at me, I said, "No one, who really knows me, would be surprised at this, but they all consider me just weird."

I have always wished I had that chart, but he wouldn't give it to me. I would have definitely framed it and kept it near as emotional support. Maybe on some plane I was a genius! Instead, I have something greater. Dr. Ed is around often as spiritual support from "over there." He comes around to visit with my childhood doctor, Dr. Hopkins.

Before that experience, my marriage ended. I can't say it failed at that point because it had been failing for years. The emotional state of the marriage had been spiraling downward, as my husband's alcohol addiction escalated. The particular night it ended brought another level of devastation into my life.

That night also marked a very low point as a parent. After I managed to get away from my husband, I found my kids barricaded in a locked bedroom with a loaded gun. They planned to protect themselves, at all cost, just in case their father decided to include them in his violence. Luckily, he was too drunk to even think about them. I would never want them to have to live with having to take their father's life to protect themselves. I think we all breathed a sigh of relief when he moved out to be with his latest girlfriend.

The neighbors helped emotionally and even bought us needed food while I tried to pull it together. I had no job and the bank accounts had been emptied. I had to build a new and completely different life for myself and my children.

While it was a very big challenge, it changed my life for the better. It was much, much harder than I imagined. When the fog eventually lifted, I knew my life had improved. I'm also convinced this is why I was offered at job at the domestic violence shelter. Boy, did I learn a lot about myself, but it also showed me where to forgive myself and help others.

As part of the healing process from that abusive marriage, I turned to metaphysical studies. I don't really know how I moved in that direction. Even in college, I had only one or two truly alternative type friends. Most of my time was spent with fellow debaters wearing regulation suit and tie, and who may have been more clueless about metaphysical world than I. We never discussed anything remotely connected to astrology, pendulums, etc., although my roommate and I did used a borrowed Ouija Board one night. There was obviously some connection somewhere, it just wasn't a conscious connection.

I think it may have heard the whir of my soul stirring when I wrote a research paper on Atlantis. I don't remember hearing of it before. Because it wasn't assigned to me, I got a lower grade. I didn't really care. The topic drew me in like a siren's song. I was fascinated. I wanted to know more about it. I'm sure there must be a connection to another life, even though I've not explored the possibility.

As I said before, I always been sensitive to energy. Whether that's natural, or I've developed the skill to stay safe, I can't say. I'm very good at picking up on the vibes of things and people. That's one reason I move furniture around until it feels right in the room. A crookedly hanging piece of art drives me wild.

I remember attending one of my husband's company parties. A man walked up, shook my hand and spoke very politely to me. Without thinking, as he turned away, I shivered. My husband was standing behind me and I said, "That man is a snake." His shocked look made me realize I had spoken out loud. When I said, "Sorry," and shrugged, he replied, "No, I'm just surprised you could tell from shaking his hand. You're right."

Many years later, and on two different occasions, I was riding in a friend's car when we passed a particular spot on a street. I immediately burst into hysterical crying and shaking. I asked, "Has a wreck occurred here?" She had grown up in that town and knew it was a fairly new street where no previous street had been. She knew of no accident at that location.

That area of the country has a history with multiple wagon train trails, mob violence, Civil War, and battles with the Plains Tribes. I must have picked up someone's imprint from a violent event. It was strong and, as I said, I had the same experience the only two times we drove over that spot. I never tried to figure it out. I really didn't want to experience someone's terrible trauma.

There are other times I felt things I would rather have not felt. I was driving home after attending my future daughter-in-law's wedding shower. I had worked until 1 a.m., slept 2 hours, gotten up, dressed, and drove from Kansas City to Dallas for the event. I was pretty tired by the time I started back home.

In the middle of Oklahoma, I felt bubbles leaving my heart and going up into my head. I got very dizzy and the landscape blurred. I pulled off the road and sat there wondering if I had just had a stroke from pushing myself to make that trip without much rest. Fortunately, the sensations passed in a couple of minutes, but I sat there a while to be sure I was okay to drive.

The doctors had performed cardiac by-pass surgery on my dad the week before. The day after my trip, I called my parent's house to check on him. Then I understood what had happened the day before. I had felt my dad having a stroke at the very time it happened.

Before then I had a very profound moment with angels. I had read a book about working with angels. I don't remember the name. It basically said, "Don't mess around. If you need an angel to do this or that, call for one." What I remembered, specifically, was the book saying, if you need a warrior angel call for a warrior, not some fluffy, soft, twinkly toed angel you've seen in artwork.

I was the Director of a private church school. When I took over the position, I had inherited a lot of power and authority issues with one of the teachers. She didn't take guidance well, or believe regulations were made for her. She decided to try and destroy the school (and me) instead of being a team player. A lot of false evidence was created and the worst of accusations were made against me, the staff and the church.

A letter was delivered to me from the state licensing agency saying that investigators would arrive by 8:00 am the following day, accompanied by law enforcement. The letter stated that if the investigators found anything even vaguely wrong, I would be arrested. You can imagine how little I slept that night.

The teachers got wind of the letter from my assistant and came collectively to tell me what had happened. They even showed me a copy of the one-inch thick "documentation" she had sent to the state agency. Every single thing in it was a lie, or something she set up for photos and then put back in place so no one would see it.

I arrived at dawn that morning to spend time in the sanctuary of the church. I spent a couple of hours praying for myself, the teachers and the school. Right before the car load of determined investigators showed up, I remembered that book. I said out loud, "God, you know I didn't do this. I need the most help I've ever needed in my life. Please send warrior angels to protect us all."

The air shifted and I clearly saw an army of angels come in and line both sides of the hallways shoulder to shoulder. As I've mentioned before, I wasn't that great at seeing the physical in the spiritual world, but it was clear that morning. The angels reminded me of pictures I had seen of Roman soldiers. The angels were as tall as the ceiling, wore helmets, chest armor and kilt-like skirts covered with a leather apron. They had on leather sandals that laced up to their knees. Each of them had a large shield and long

spear. They were massively built.

I was so grateful that they showed up. It was impressive and a bit scary to see them fill the church and to feel their power. It was confirmation to me, that the highest powers that be knew the truth and would help me. I learned that day, though, the book was right. Don't pussyfoot around when you need something. *ASK!*

The teachers and I went through 9 hours of interrogation and inspections with those angels standing there emanating their power. Of course, that problem person had called in sick that day, but in the long run it was a blessing. The long tense day ended with the lead investigator apologizing for what they had put us through. She handed me the complaint paperwork saying, "I can't tell you who did this to you, but I think you can figure it out."

I called on angels in new ways after that day. Many years later I opened a massage therapy office. It was in that same town where I had experienced the melt down while driving with my friend. Between me calling in angels and other spirits showing up, it was a busy place.

I found my license on the floor two days in a row. I asked the woman who rented the other room if she had taken a book off the shelf where was license was and maybe accidently knocked it down. I really thought that might be the explanation. She said, "No." As she was saying no, together, we watched as my license once again floated to the floor. I looked at it and realized it was nearly time to get my continuing education hours into the state for renewal. Spirit was watching the calendar for me.

Sometimes amusing things happened in that office.

I had painted a large land-scape for the front waiting room. One of my clients, who was also a friend, asked me where the fairies were. "What do you mean?" I asked. "Show me where you painted the fairies," she replied. I tried to assure her I didn't paint any fairies, but she got a bit snippy and demanded that I show her the fairies. There was nothing I could do to satisfy her. I shrugged it off until... A couple weeks later I saw another client up close peering at the

painting. I asked what she was doing and she replied, "Looking for the fairies." With raised eyebrows, I replied, "I didn't paint fairies into the landscape." As she opened her mouth to protest, I raised my hand to stop her, saying, "There may be fairies in there because you aren't the first person to look for them, but I didn't paint any fairies." Fairies must have liked the landscape scene and moved in.

Someone offered to buy that painting more than once. I just couldn't bring myself to sell the fairies' home.

I had never considered a bunch of fairies could live in one of my paintings, but I've certainly learned what is considered reality isn't, so why not? Remember, years later I and a friend saw a fairy in the flesh. I still feel one flutter in the corners of rooms sometimes.

This year, a couple of days before my grandson's birthday, I was doing my daily channeling with Spirit and felt that flutter in the corner. Then a box of fairy oracle cards suddenly fell off a stack of card deck boxes. It had been there for a while. I contemplated whether or not I had caused that fall, but concluded there was no way I had made the box fall, nor was it off balance on the stack so that any vibration might have cause the fall.

I decided the fairies must have a message for me. I opened the box up. I shuffled the cards and drew one. I burst into laughter as I read the explanation in the book for that card. It said (paraphrasing) you may not be paying attention and might miss someone's birthday. I put the cards back, stopped what I was doing and sent my grandson's birthday gift a few days early. The fairies apparently thought I might forget, so I didn't want to take any chances.

I still don't know what the message was, but while I had the massage therapy office, I had strong encounters with a red hawk that lasted over several weeks. There was a clover leaf intersection to exit the main highway and take another highway into town. One day I was barreling along going to the office when suddenly a very large red hawk dive bombed my car. It scared me enough to physically dodge it in my car and let out a bit of a scream. For several days the same thing happened, leaving me wondering why that hawk hated my car, instead of realizing he must have a message he was trying to deliver. He seemed to just dive down from the heavens because all the trees had been cleared when they built the big intersection over the past year or so.

Then the hawk moved to a new position, apparently still determined to get my attention. As I would drive down the street to the office, he would dive bomb me from a tree. I didn't get it and really didn't try to see it as a spiritual message. As I said, I didn't know much about animal communication. I'm sure I missed out on a special growth opportunity, but I just didn't get it.

I told my hawk story to the therapist who had witnessed my license floating to the floor. She clearly thought I was telling tall tales, so I didn't pursue the story. However, old red hawk came through for me.

Twice a year a big gem and mineral show came to town. The therapist, one of her clients and I were going to the show together. The even was just a few days after I told her about the hawk. I was driving down the same street. Bless his heart, that hawk saw us coming and dive bombed the car right toward that doubting therapist who was sitting in the front passenger seat of my car. She screamed and practically dove under the dashboard. She just looked at me, smirking at her and finally said, "I didn't believe you." I must admit, I rubbed it in a bit

I'm still not great at receiving physical animal messages, but a friend's cat did sing to me. I'm sure that was another part of the frazzle, opening my eyes and ears to possibilities with physical animals. I do see and receive messages from animals in spirit Apparently, they follow me about.

I attended a Dallas medium's Spirit Gallery. He started off by asking, "Who lives on a ranch?" No one did. I raised my hand and said, "I live in a ranching area, but not on a ranch." He then told me all the animals had come to the gallery with me. He said, "The room is absolutely filled with horses, cattle, and goats, etc. By the way, you also have a unicorn standing next to you." I have no idea why they came or how they knew me, but Spirit works in mysterious ways, right? I think, though, the spirit of the equine may have been calling to me.

One day, the Trail Boss of a trail ride group walked into my work office. He asked me to ride along with them to report about their activities for the newspaper. I declined for various reasons, including a couple of traumatic experiences with horses. What

I said out loud was, "I don't think so. I'm not a cowgirl kind of person." He insisted that didn't matter, but I declined anyway. He came back again. Thinking of a new excuse, I said, "I don't have a horse." He insisted he had several and I could ride one of his. I declined. He came back again. I looked at him while frantically trying to think of another excuse. Instead, I thought, "He is going to come back until I agree to go." So, with trepidation, I agreed to go, but only if I could ride in a wagon.

When I arrived for my first trail ride, someone was assigned to help me. He turned to me and asked, "Do you want to ride in the money wagon?" I looked at him and replied, "I have no idea what that means, but if there is a money wagon, I certainly want to ride in it!"

Riding with the group became a bright spot in my life. During one ride, I even learned to be a mule skinner and drive a covered wagon-the Money Wagon. It turned out that wagon belonged to the Money family who spent a lot of time trail riding together.

I began to see the trail ride horses respond to my thoughts. They began to break training to come over to me and rub some love on me. They made me laugh. When the music was blasting out the back of the wagon they danced with their heads in time with the music. When they saw my camera, I swear they posed for me.

The horses became an important part of opening my heart to other types of love. They helped me realize that, if necessary, Spirit's messengers will literally walk in the door over and over until you just give up control and go along with what you are meant to learn. You don't get just one opportunity. Spirit offers do-overs.

I met so many wonderful people. When we rode in parades, the amount of love people threw at us was heart-breaking (in a good way). I am forever grateful to that old cowboy who wouldn't take no for an answer.

The best gift of it all was that the experience opened my heart to the spirit of those horses and brought an understand of that loving community. I believe that Trail Boss was used as one of Spirit's guides to expand my dazzle in the Universe *and* I had some very interesting stories to create for the newspaper with my photography and writing.

For a few years, I received sonar pings from objects and people. If they happen now, I don't notice it, but it could be my guidance is teaching me other things. Those pings were useful, though. I was shopping in a preschool supply store when a bell for a baby pinged me. It wasn't anything unusual. It had a loop handle and a bell-shaped cage that contained the actual bell. As my daughter was newly pregnant, I bought it and put it away. When I sent it to her, she wasn't particularly impressed with the bell, but it turned out to be my grandson's favorite baby toy. He even made up a game to play with it.

Another time a statue in a friend's yard pinged me as I walked out the front door of their house. It came up later in a conversation, so I knew exactly what statue she was referencing in her story. We were going out for dinner. From the back seat of the car she asked, "You know that..." Before she completed her sentence, I replied, "Uh huh." She continued. She was intuitive so she had no problem with what happened. However, her partner was stunned at the lack of conversation, but complete understanding we had.

Perhaps the most interesting event occurred while a friend was styling my hair. A week before, she had told me she might be pregnant. As I sat in the stylist's chair, a very strong ping hit me from her uterus. I looked at her in the mirror and said, "You definitely have a baby in there. It just pinged me." She was pleased, but we were both surprised the baby reached out like that.

I joined a Master Mind group after I met one of its members during a Matrix Energetics training. I was in a hotel ballroom in Dallas, Texas, when man sat down beside me. He said he thought I looked like someone he should sit next to. In training like that, you know what he said wasn't a pick-up line. He really felt he should sit down. It turned out we both lived in the Kansas City area. He invited me into the Master Mind group. It was comprised of people were intuitive and worked with energy.

The Master Mind Group decided to do an energy experiment. One of the members had had a vision of a circle of people sending energy with a gatekeeper standing outside the circle. They were creating a torus field. We planned to reenact that vision. We needed thirteen people. (Remember 13 people raising energy at the birthday luncheon?) We only had six in our group. Once we asked an owner of a yoga studio if we could use her facility, it didn't take long to fine more participants.

We gathered at the studio and arranged twelve chairs in as large a circle as we could. The person with the vision was to be the the 13th person and gatekeeper. He decided who would sit where and how the energy should be sent across the circle, based on what he saw in his vision.

We got off to a bad start. We started sending energy *at* each other. We might have knocked our socks off, only we were barefooted. We had to stop, clear the energy, and pull ourselves together. After discussion we realized our error. We began again just pulling energy through ourselves and sending it into the center of the circle, not *at* each other.

What I saw that day is etched into my forever memory. As the energy poured into the circle, it began to form a sphere. Then, what looked like soccer balls began to form and bounce around inside the sphere as though we were creating new universes.

Later, what I assumed was a shaman rode the energy down into the circle. He was dressed in a short skirt with fringe, leggings, a short sleeveless shirt, and a large feather headdress. The shaman moved about the circle with a rattle going around to each of us. I'm not sure if he was blessing us or healing us, but he attended each person. He then rode the energy back up and out of the building.

The group stopped again to rest and discuss our experiences. We each wrote prayers and placed them in the center of our circle. When we began running energy again, glowing beings came and sat cross-legged between each chair. I wasn't sure what they were doing until I felt one of my hands being adjusted to aim the energy into a different spot. Most of us saw our prayers being lifted by the energy. It was a sacred day.

There have been times when I had clear telepathy with various family members. They would give me shocked looks when I responded to their thoughts. They might argue they never said a word to me, but would admit to thinking in silence what I said they spoke. One night as I was cutting drapery fabric, I heard my daughter say, "Mommy, my tummy is hurting." I got up and went down the hall to check on her. I found her, still asleep, but curled into a ball clutching her stomach.

I heard a friend, who is highly intuitive, wonder what I was doing while I was running energy and merging with pink quartz. Apparently, he felt the shift in my energy and tapped in, so I heard his thought. One friend recently told me that she tries to clear her mind about me so I won't telepathically pick up if she is going to contact me. I'm definitely not trying to read anyone's mind, but it can happen. We had a good laugh over what she was doing, though. I can feel certain people reading online posts and emails, or even someone focusing on me to leave me a note. I just acknowledge the energy connection without trying to be invasive.

I have often experienced a knowing about things, plus those times the messages came tumbling out of my mouth that I spoke of earlier. I occasionally heard someone I couldn't see say, "Hello Lillie," in the most melodious voice. I saw things in my head and more rarely with my eyes. Walking in the woods gave me the creeps because I felt everything watching me. Just being in a room with certain people could give me migraines from their energy. I have even developed severe colds in just a couple of hours from picking up negative energy emanating from someone. I developed cysts in my breasts from the negativity with my husband. I realized that was the source of the cysts after they completely disappeared within weeks of him moving out of our house. (I've never had one since.) I was often drained by people I encountered and avoided shopping malls like they were akin to a Biblical plague. I found them exhausting. I spent a lot of time learning how to take care of myself energetically.

As you now know, I never formally studied any of the spiritual phenomenon I experienced early in life, nor did I admit it existed in me. Growing up, it wasn't safe to even mention it. That was viewed as devil stuff, apparently, even though it was how God made me.

That attitude was rather curious, though, as there was this interesting story told about my great grandmother. Maybe, in some ways, I *had* been exposed to the idea of spiritual messages as a young child without realizing it.

In the early 20th century, my great uncle built a carbide lamp. Carbide lamps burn acetylene gas. That gas is now commonly found in welding shops that use acetylene gas torches. Also known as calcium carbide, it is very dangerous when it is wet. Today it's restricted as a hazardous material.

As the story goes, my great grandmother was afraid of the lamp and began to get very agitated, insisting, "Get that thing out of here. It's going to kill somebody." Apparently, Great Grandma was having a premonition. To make her happy, Great Uncle Walter carried it outside. It happened to be storming that day or night. Walter carried the lamp into the yard. While you might think he got it wet causing an explosion, actually lightning struck and he died.

No one knows if the lightning struck the ground, Walter, or

the lamp. It really didn't matter. Between the explosion of the lamp and the lightning strike, Walter was killed. Great Grandma was right. That lamp *was* going to kill someone, whether it was directly caused by the lamp or not. From a couple of things my grandmother said, I don't think her mother ever got over the event. I can't say how easily I would recover either. So, there is a possibility that "knowing" runs in the family. However, the things I experienced as a child were more likely to have taught me to tune into higher aspects of spirituality in addition to natural gifts.

At less than one year old, I was allowed to almost drown to teach me a lesson. My family was fishing at my grandparents' fishing lake. I was fascinated by the minnows around the dock as any baby would be. As they flashed prettily in the water, I was trying to reach for them. I was warned by my mother to move back, or I would fall into the water. I couldn't comprehend that idea as a baby and those shiny minnows were alluring. Sure enough, I fell in because I was allowed to fall in. My mother let me stay on the bottom of the lake until I nearly drowned. Proudly, Mom often told that story, and repeated how she had taught me a lesson about, "Doing as I was told." I was traumatized.

I never learned to swim very well. I claimed I had passed the swimming test to get out of more lessons that required I put my face in the water. It was too reminiscent of nearly drowning.

As a child, I remember fighting the anesthesiologist before surgery. Both times he put that mask over my face, I couldn't breathe and I felt I was drowning again. I remember trying to thrash away from the doctors standing around the surgery table, crying out, "No, please don't!"

The results of that "lesson" even ruined a chance for me to snorkel in Hawaii. I had looked forward to seeing all the brightly colored fish for weeks. We jumped off the tour boat and floated over near the coral reefs. Even though the snorkel provided air and the mask protected my eyes, I just couldn't put my face down into the ocean water. As soon as I tried, I had a panic attack and began gasping for air. It felt too close to nearly drowning. I've wondered, at times, if that near drowning isn't why I have asthma, or at least part of the reason. When the humidity is high, my lungs hurt.

I had been frequently told my throat chakra needs balancing. I think that energy center still struggles, not only for air, but also from having my voice suppressed as a child. Asking a question, or more importantly, telling the truth about some event, or situation, was a sure way to have my face slapped to shut my mouth. I also had to keep silent about the abuse if I didn't want, "More of the same." I made the mistake, once, of telling my grandmother why I was crying and showing her the full hand print mark on my leg. After she got on to my mom, I was punished even more harshly. I learned not to seek help.

I still don't enjoy getting my hair cut. When the stylist's comb gets stuck on a snarl and it hurts, I am taken back to my mother's hand striking like a snake and pulling my hair as hard as she could. Brushing my hair was equally painful. The more I cried, the more roughly I was treated.

I was severely burned twice as a toddler. The first time it was my right arm and hand. In less than a year, I was burned on my left arm and leg.

An interesting bit of serendipity occurred with one of my burn scars. I had a very rough and wrinkled scar that covered most of the outside of my left thigh. I was bitten by something, possibly a spider, right in the center of that scar. I was given a bottle of Calamine Lotion to put on the burning and itching bite. Even though that scar swelled up, turned red, and was inflamed for a number of days, I wasn't taken to the doctor. I simply treated it myself. However, when it finally healed, the scar was no longer rippled up with the bands of scar tissue underneath the skin. The scar was almost flat. I think God had a hand in using that bite to smooth the scar tissue, so I would no longer be bullied about the scar during gym class.

As you know, my school mates weren't the only bullies in my life. My brother, with his size, easily intimidated Mom. I received several pretty severe beatings as she flipped out to protect herself from him. I was then required to use the money I made babysitting to replace coat hangers, brushes, belts or whatever else she had broken across my back. While it was wrong, I know he frightened her. She was trying to protect herself from him. However, as I mentioned, she had her own ways of bullying, too, including a lot of caustic remarks and emotional abuse. Dad also used me as a scape goat to avoid my brother's intimidation.

My family provided a lot of traumatic drama in my life. My young psyche seemed to be stuck forever riding a Tilt-o-Whirl. I never knew what direction life would spin next. There was no center of gravity to my life. I all could do was hold on and try not to throw up.

As I said before, this isn't a victim story. I mention these things because, later, some of the events, had a special place in my life as that spider bite did. Some of them helped me developed the skills I have today.

Learning to disassociate from the pain of punishment and rejection can have a serendipitous result. Being able to disassociate from my body meant allowing energy to flow through me during Reiki training was a snap. It has, however, made staying here on earth and connected to my body challenging.

I was locked in a closet as a baby by my older brother. When I was finally found and released from the closet, the fear of the dark never left me. I think being locked in that closet might have brought back a past life memory. Since I was only around a year old, there is no way of knowing for certain. I bring this event up because many years later, while on a vacation in another country, I had a spontaneous reliving of a life where I was buried alive. It happened two nights in a row. After that, I wasn't *as* afraid of the dark.

I believe part of my discomfort with the dark comes from feeling things that I can't see. It's probably comes into play with the creepiness I feel in the forest too. As I've grown to see and process more spiritually, the fear has waned a good deal. At any rate, that spontaneous reliving of such an experience while on vacation in New Zealand made the idea of past lives, and "life everlasting," real to me. It was no longer just something I read in a book, or heard about at church. However, I changed my mind about lives being in the past. I will discuss that later.

I've had people tell me the life I relived must have been in New Zealand, but I don't think so. I was sleeping in the loft of a camper. It was late fall there and cool at night. As heat rises, it got very hot up in the camper loft. I woke up desperately gasping for air and thinking I was buried alive. As I fought to breathe and was processing that memory, I managed to hang over the edge of the loft and suck in some cooler air. As I lay back on the bed, I remembered forgiving the people who had buried me. I remembered being sick and, I suppose, in a coma. Whomever had buried me thought I had died. I knew they didn't know better, not that they meant me harm. Apparently, that was before the days of safety coffins, or being saved by the bell.

The exact same thing occurred the next night while I was sleeping in the camper. I think it had more to do with the loft being about the size of a coffin, dark and windowless, than where we were vacationing. Then, it got hot again and, apparently, I did not have enough oxygen in that space. I think the similar circumstances threw me back into that life as the dark closet might have. As a toddler, I had no way of processing what occurred me, *if*, there is any relationship between the two things.

I just know I wasn't *as* afraid of the dark after that trip to New Zealand. At any rate, many things, such as that event, have added to what I might be aware of from time to time and my ability to live my life through psychic sensitivity.

If you have remembered other lives, as I have, it makes the idea of a soul family plausible. I imagine that if you look back through your life, you will find someone that you had a special and close relationship with whom you, "just hit it off." That person is likely someone you knew "over there."

I had a friend that had to have been part of my soul family. Sadly, she passed away just days before I started this story. We met through the Midwest Center for Nonprofit Leadership. We quickly realized we had a mutual interest in other realms.

On one occasion, we went together to a small psychic fair. A man selling books said something about us being sisters. We denied the connection and we looked nothing alike. He didn't believe us. He focused on our energy and insisted we were sisters and that we were trying to fool him. I think he was reading the soul family connection and was unable to see it didn't apply to our earthly lives. He was still insisting we were sisters when we finally walked away from him shaking our heads. At the same fair, another vendor strangely got up from his table with an inquisitive look on his face. He started following us around the room. He was creeping us out. It turned out he, too, thought we were a sister act and was reading our energy for some reason. We never knew what he was actually doing, but we steered clear of him. While there have been other people to whom I have strongly connected and suspect that we have had other life connections, one event sure took me by surprise.

I was strolling along through a shopping center parking lot headed into Borders Bookstore. I saw a woman with her toddler in her arms. He looked to be nearly two years old. He must have known me from other realms. As I passed by them, his face lit up. He squirmed in his mother's arms to stare at me as I walked past. Then I heard very clearly in my head, "Hey! Hey! How *are* you?" He sounded delighted to see me after some length of time. I have no idea who he or his mother are, nor have I ever seen them again. He clearly recognized me from somewhere and his soul spoke to me telepathically.

XIV

Some of the things that either started happening as I worked on opening up my senses, or that simply came into my awareness, just couldn't be denied. I was all over the place, though. No clear path emerged, at least that I recognized. I thought my life was all about the frazzle. I was still looking for what I considered would be my dazzle.

After my husband walked out of the family, my daughter and I would go to the bookstore to help heal the pain. We read a *lot* of books to get us through this hard time, and I even had an informal self-help book trading group with friends. One particular day, I was drawn to the alternative health section. I had had an interest in natural health for a long time. A brown book kept luring me to pull it off the shelf. I looked at it a couple of times, but I was clueless what it was about. I put it back at least twice, but it kept pulling at me. So, I bought it thinking I would figure out what it was about, later. As we left the store, my daughter pulled my books out of the sack and asked, "What's this?" I replied I had no idea. She asked, "Why did you buy it?" I replied again that I had no idea. She gave me that look that says, "Crazy lady on board."

For two or three weeks, I would take out that book, flip through it, and afterwards, still be as clueless about the content as I had been before buying it. Then, one day, I went to pick up the mail. There was a letter from a local psychic we knew. She was inviting us to a class to be held in her home. It was to be given by a friend of the psychic who needed some human guinea pigs. The friend was offering a weekend training in something called Reiki. Reiki was practically unheard of nearly thirty years ago. I certainly didn't know what it was, *but* that book I bought? Yep, you guessed it, <u>Essential Reiki</u>. It was one of the first, if not the first, book on Reiki. It was also the textbook for the class! After the weekend was over, I finally knew what the book was about!

My daughter and I took the training and that opened up my spiritual channels even more. While it was all interesting, and it all helped me get to know my *real* self better (The one I had kept hidden for safety), I still didn't focus much on it. I had to put food on the table. Spirituality and Reiki were more of a side-line interest. Later, I took the other level classes and became a Reiki Master.

I also realized that, years before, I had naturally done some Reiki type healing work on my son. He had developed Swimmer's Ear from a trip to the beach. I had him lay his head in my lap, and I put my hand over his ear. I didn't know I was sending his ear balancing energy. I just "knew" it would make it feel better, and it did. No wonder Spirit led me to that book and the class. It was a way to refine what I was naturally doing.

A number of years later, I decided I wanted to learn more about how energy effects the physical body. I enrolled in a program and earned an AA degree in massage therapy. I know it may seem backwards for someone already having a Bachelor's Degree and some Master's hours, but that's what I did.

I lived in a state that required a national certification to practice massage therapy. Once I had that license, I needed a lot of continuing education units. I used that requirement as a reason to be certified in all types of energy work. While I provided massage therapy, I also provided energy work to my clients. All of that opened spiritual connections even more, but I still didn't know what I wanted to be when I grew up. I was now more frazzled than ever. I enjoyed being a therapist, but something seemed missing.

Metaphysics increasingly became more important in my life. I also focused more on working with angels, but some days I felt they just weren't focusing back on me. Then, after some whining from me, they would hit me with their best shot. One day, I was fussing to my angels saying, "I need you to be *obvious*. If you are giving me signs and messages, I'm not getting them.

Later that day, the door opened at my massage business. A lady walked in looking rather scared. She held out a brochure and said, "I was buying gas across the street. I don't know why, but I have to give you this." The brochure was about angels. I laughed and told her I had asked my angels to be obvious with their messages. I thanked her for delivering the message, but she still left with a be-fuddled look on her face.

Now, what are the odds some lady buying gas had that brochure in her car in the first place, or that her urge to come to a strange place was so strong she brought that message to me from my angels? My angels had delivered exactly what I was asking for, an obvious message.

Things were certainly opening up for me, but not as much as I would have liked. However, you get out what you put in. I was waiting for the big *it* to come while Spirit was waiting for me to understand frazzle is dazzle.

Despite that, I was having some crazy experiences. One even ended up on the National UFO Reporting Center website. The few people I told about the event tried to convince me I had a dream. I didn't. At least Peter Davenport who has been Director of the National UFO Reporting Center since 1994 believed me. I'm sure my experience wasn't the least bit surprising to him in his line of work.

After I made the report, Mr. Davenport called me. I imagine he wanted to make sure I wasn't a kook. His main question was, "Why did you wait so long to report it?"

It took several years for me to report the event: 1. I didn't know the reporting center existed; 2. No one I previously told had believed me; 3. Every single one of my friends to whom I told the story, tried to convince me I was dreaming. It was the only filter they had because they had never experienced anything like what I described. It still discouraged me from sharing the information.

This event, however, was no ghostly event. For me, it was a purely physical experience. That is, if you call watching your bedroom wall turn into what looked like ripples in a pond, physical. I watched, what appeared to be a spy ball pass right through the rippling wall. I ran into the room on the other side of the wall, but there was no spy ball. Although it had flown into my bedroom through the hallway door and was moving about, looking me over, it disappeared when it went through the wall. I didn't sleep very much that night.

The day I walked through some guy in a hat in my bathroom was too much though. I yelled at him to get out and said it was just too creepy to be walking through people. I think he must have been a remote viewer because he didn't feel like any ghostly spirit I've felt.

I have no idea how those two events played into my other sensory development, if so. It could just be that my energy and all the energy work I was doing in the house simply alerted some governmental agency.

I thought those events were restricted to the area I lived in and to that time in my life because nothing else happened, at least that I noticed. Then about fifteen years later, and in a different location that was nine hundred miles away, I was awakened by an energy beam coming into the hallway. It moved through the bedroom door and then slowly scanned me as I lay scared to death in my bed. I didn't jump up and run away, I was frozen in fear.

As I said, I have no idea if those events had anything to do with the growth of my sensing, but I suppose I wouldn't have been aware of them without being able to sense energy. The spy ball experience wass entirely different and so was a friend's cell phone.

I traveled to Iowa to visit a friend. It was a pleasant two-hour drive. Later in the day, I was channeling and autotyping information to her questions. Although she was asking the questions, she was sometimes skeptical of the answers. She watched and read the answers as I worked.

Whenever, she expressed doubt about the information I received, her cell phone would ring. Each time the caller id showed the number #0-000-000-0000. We both saw the calerl id number. She tried to answer, but of course, no one was there. Her phone rang at other times during the time I was visiting. It never showed the zeros again because I wasn't channeling and she wasn't doubting Spirit's answers to her questions.

 I'm not sure what all was happening during that time of my spiritual growth, but things were changing. One day while meditating, I freaked out. I saw a black panther walk through my living room. Luckily, it was in spirit and apparently, not hungry. Maybe that was because I lived a block away from what is considered a very haunted cemetery, or maybe not. That was a couple of weeks after Tiger, my friend from Iowa's cat, walked the same path through my living room, also during meditation. He was a spirit traveling, but he

wasn't dead. As I said, I'm not sure what all was happening, but I am sure that some if it definitely seemed strange.

I'd read about events like I was experiencing in books, but only kind of, sort of, believed, but yet didn't disbelieve either. As these things began happening though, the reality of that type of occurrence was hard to deny. Looking back, there were some hints that could have taken away the surprise, if I had known known more about numerology. The street number of that house was 7000 and my Life path number is 7. Seven is the number for awakening spiritual gifts and connecting with others on a spiritual level.

I briefly joined an online psychic development group. I still can't logically explain what happened. An exercise was set up so members could volunteer for people to give them past life readings.

I had never given a past life reading, so I decided to give it a try. I picked out a lady's name from the list. I received very detailed information about a life she had lived. That life took place in an ancient part of India that no longer exists because it sunk under the ocean. It's been so long ago, I don't remember all the details, but part of the information had to do with riding elephants and a special jewel she wore over her third eye. During that life, the lady was some sort of royalty in that nation. I wrote about the movie that played in my head where I saw her riding the elephant through adoring throngs of people. Then, I sent the reading information to her.

I received an email back from her that sounded rather angry. She demanded to know how I had gotten her name and email address. I explained I took her name from the list of volunteers in the group. She emphatically stated that she had never heard of the group, was not a member, and had not signed up for a reading. I asked if maybe a friend had volunteered her, but she stated she knew no one in the group. Then she said, "Ever since I read your email my third eye has been throbbing!"

I looked at the list of volunteers again and she wasn't there.

Sure enough, she wasn't on the membership list either. I never heard from her again, but I decided to attempt one more reading.

This reading was about a lady getting chased by squirrels into the back of the pickup truck in another life. I don't remember the rest of it, but I heard, "This is for April." I couldn't find an April on the list of volunteers. After my other experience in this group, I hesitated. Finally, I posted it under the heading "For April. I couldn't find you, but that's the name they gave me."

A couple of days later, and as I was driving into the garage after work, I got a strong feeing someone had answered my post. Sure enough, I had a response, "Hi, this is April. I didn't use my real name because I wanted the right person to find me."

It turned out April had an angel store in another state and her own online group. She also confirmed my information about being chased into the pickup truck by squirrels. She asked me to do readings for her group. I spent the next 2-3 years giving past life readings for people through her group.

I now call readings, such as that type reading, Other Life Readings. I no longer believe we have past lives, but that they are happening all at the same time and we move in and out of them, sometimes overlapping timelines. I came to that conclusion during a meditation during a mediumship class.

While I was deep in that meditation, a spirit came. She was dressed in a similar fashion as an ancient Grecian in the soft, thin, flowy fabrics you see on carvings or ancient pottery. She partially melded her energy with mine. As I was processing her arrival, I realized she was me in another time. What really grabbed my attention was that I could feel her heart beat. It was beating just a fraction of a second differently from mine, so I detected it. How could I feel her heart beating if she was dead? From that moment on, I changed my philosophy on past lives to believing in other lives.

I think those overlapping lives and time lines could explain the doppelganger too. A doppelganger is an apparition or double of a living person. Yes, I had an experience with one of those too. The children and I were driving to a mall. As we approached an intersection, we saw my husband's red pickup truck. He was driving and a woman was in the passenger's seat. He was in the left turn lane. We were going straight. That put us right beside each other. We honked and waved, but they looked at us with no recognition. We honked and waved some more, with no return waves or recognition.

After we returned home, I called my husband at work and demanded to know why he had ignored us. He was confused and insisted he had not left the office since lunch time. I had a hard time believing him, but I hadn't thought to check the license plate of the identical red truck. I had serious doubts it wasn't him, but I let it go.

About two weeks later, and after a snowfall, I took our van to wash off the road salt. I had finished spraying it off and had climbed back in to leave. I looked forward and sat in stunned silence.

There in front of me was an identical red pickup truck and a man who could have, literally, been an identical twin brother to my husband. He was slightly shorter and stouter, but generally the same size. His face and hair were almost identical. So identical that I had to look closely to be sure my husband hadn't somehow gotten to the car wash to vacuum his truck in less time than it took for me to drive there. The man was dressed for the cool weather in exactly the same shirt my husband had on when I left the house for the car wash. As I sat there, I realized what had happened near the mall. I had seen this man who, apparently, lived in the same Kansas town as we did.

A number of years later, I was watching the clouds while sitting at the park and eating my lunch. There were tall trees on either side of the street. From my view point the sky was framed in green on the left and right sides. I watched as an airplane started across the sky from my right to my left. When the airplane traveled over to the left side of my framed in view, it was suddenly all the way back to the right. It repeated going across the sky a second time. I watched it fly across the sky a second time in stunned silence. My mouth hung open awaiting my next bite, and my hands clutched my hamburger half way to my lips. That few seconds of history had repeated itself right in front of my eyes, but the plane was now in a different time by a second or two.

It makes you think about how times and lives really work, doesn't it? It certainly makes you rethink that phrase, "History repeats itself." With all of this, I was becoming more and more frazzled, or maybe diversified, in what I could do. Still, I was clueless about the final chapter, or if there was one, called Dazzle.

Another event took place on one of those perfect autumn days. The trees were brilliant that year. The city was filled with bright orange and yellow leaves that shown in that special sunlight October seems to always have. The temperature was perfect. I was at a traffic light on a street that dead-ended on the other side of the cemetery that was a block from where I lived. I looked across the intersection toward the cemetery and got the best view I've ever had of spirits. The bus bench was filled with spirits all dressed up, reminding me of the fashions of the 1940s and 1950s. There were several spirits standing behind the bench. I could tell they were enjoying that perfect fall day.

I thought that might be it, finally. Now, I could see spirits! It didn't last long though. While I can occasionally see spirits, I mostly hear them and feel them. It was just another piece of that unknown puzzle that seemed to frazzle into nothingness. Meanwhile, weirdness continued to be part of my life, but it was becoming more the norm. Frankly, I was mesmerized and delighted by most of it.

While I was too busy to pay much attention, some of the pesky child spirits who had plagued me for several years came along when I moved back home to tend to my mother's illnesses. About fifteen years before, and while living in Kansas, I would be woken up from a sound sleep by a very loud doorbell ringing in the middle of the night. My adrenaline would wildly pump, keeping me awake for a while. It was annoying, especially if it happened more than once a night. When I moved across the state line into Missouri, I thought I had left those little spirits behind. However, when that doorbell, that did not exist in the one-hundred-year-old home I lived in, rang several times waking me up, I knew the child spirits had come along for the move. Even when I moved nearly 900 miles away, they would still wake me up ringing that doorbell.

I guess after all that time, the spirit children were growing bolder. I had to practically peel my pounding heart off the ceiling when I was awakened by what sounded like a bunch of pipes being dropped. I heard the spirit children's giggles and groaned. The next time they tried the pipe drop, I put on my best angry mom voice and chewed them out. Thank goodness that worked.

It didn't keep a boy spirit named Stephen from opening my closet in the middle of the night, though. The closet had one of those lights that comes on when the door is opened. About 3:00 am seemed to be his favorite time to open the door. Being awakened at that time of the morning did not help me stay awake at work. It did, however, provide an evening of comic relief.

My dad had a lot of strict rules everyone had to abide by. One of those involved turning off lights. I had given Stephen instructions that he wasn't to open the door in the middle of the night any more. I had to get some rest for work. He moved his antics to early evening.

I was sitting watching television where I could easily see into the part of my bedroom where the closet was. I saw the light come on and knew Stephen was following instructions not to play around in the middle of the night.

Dad grumbled about me leaving on lights and wasting electricity. I told him the door wouldn't stay shut. I didn't dare say, "There's a ghost named Stephen in my closet and it's his fault." I'm sure Dad would have thought I ran around in one of those little tin foil hats and was ready for check-in at a mental health facility. He certainly would have thought I was lying about leaving lights turned on.

Dad had to prove to himself that I was simply negligent in closing the door. Remember now, I could see everything happening and I was silently laughing as the events transpired.

Dad traipsed into my room and firmly shut the closet door. He turned and took a couple of steps to leave. Stephen opened the door again. Dad stopped, then, returned to the closet. He shut the door firmly again, pushed on it a bit and jiggled the knob to be sure it was closed. Again, he took a couple of steps to leave. The room lit up as Stephen, again, opened the door. Dad froze. He slowly turned and went back to the closet. This time he shut the door a couple of times, jiggled it, pushed against it and then stood staring at the knob for several seconds waiting for it to open. The closet stayed firmly shut until just about the time he got into the hallway to return to his chair. As Dad entered the hallway, I saw the light come back on. I guess Dad gave up at that point because he never said another word. Later, I told Stephen his fun was over. He had to move on. He did.

Those aren't the only spirits who have visited, of course. Plenty of family members come around. I've even had my ex husband's family come to visit. His uncle played with the lights on cue to verify a message I had heard from him.

While I always got my keys back, sometimes they don't return things. I had a client whose husband, an amateur rock hound, had passed away. She brought me one of the stones he had mined, a fire opal. It was beautiful, but it kept disappearing. It would be gone a while and then be right back in the obvious spot it occupied on the shelf. It finally disappeared for good. I believe he didn't want her to give it away and finally just kept it. Who knows? It might have ended up back in her garage. It was a thoughtful gesture, regardless.

I took some mediumship classes from several area-based people. I was getting better at receiving information. It also gen-erated other unusual experiences, but still no "you are this" mo-ment.

When I had taken Matrix Energetics training years before, the instructors had talked about someone going into the carpet.

While that may seem far-fetched to some of you, I can assure it's not. I was sitting in a mediumship class given by a very famous psychic/medium in the Unity Church Pyramid in Houston, Texas, when yet another interesting experience took place.

During a meditation, I felt my right leg start becoming just bits of energy disintegrating and going down into the floor. I dissolved nearly to my knee and it seemed as though it would keep going until my leg was just vibration instead of matter. As I was mentally observing that interesting phenomenon and thinking about the story of the woman who went into the carpet, my left leg started dissolving and going into the floor, too. I forced myself to pull back and become solid again. "What if I get stuck in the floor?" I thought, "They might not know and there I would be living in the pyramid's floor."

The US Navy's Philadelphia Experiment came to mind. Men were reported to have ended up with their bodies stuck halfway in walls etc. My legs dissolving and going through the floor was a strange experience, but it more than convinced me things like being stuck in the walls or floor on the USS Eldridge could happen.

Less dramatic, but equally curious, something happened on a Memorial Day. I'm sure, I spent the day going back and forth from one dimension to another.

I had rescued a commercial doll cradle from being thrown away. I planned to refinish it and give it to my granddaughters. Other than some misguided attempts at refinishing the cradle, it was in perfect condition. It just looked nasty so it was being thrown out. I lugged the cradle outside that Memorial Day. I got to work stripping off the misapplied varnish. As I went outside with the cradle, I noticed the air had an odd yellow cast to it. The air was completely still. I shrugged it off, but as the day wore on, I began to wonder if I was moving from one dimension to another.

I lived on a cul-de-sac. From six houses, there were fourteen children of various ages. All the families got along well and were frequently out in the street talking and having fun. At the least, someone would be driving in and out of the street several times a day, especially when it was a long holiday weekend. Our cul-de-sac ran parallel to a much busier connecting street. Yet, no one seemed to be at home in a pretty large subdivision much less going anywhere.

I worked outside on the cradle for most of the day. I saw no one. I heard no one, No dog barked. No bird chirped. No one on our street came outside. There was no noise coming from inside the houses. Not a single car drove down the parallel connector or the street our cul-de-sac connected to. There was no wind as there usually was. It was as though the houses and community were empty.

I have some Irish ancestry. From that lineage, I am fair skinned and usually develop a sunburn quickly. After nearly the entire day outside, I wasn't even a bit tanned, much less pink from the sun.

It felt so strange to be in a place that looked normal, but clearly wasn't. I went back and forth into the house a few times, just to verify that something was different outside. Inside the house everything was normal. The answering machine had recorded several calls. The clocks showed the day was progressing. I was hearing normal noises in the house. Outside, it was eerie silence in a yellow haze. I kept expecting to hear, "You are about to enter another dimension. A dimension not only of sight and sound, but of mind. A journey into a wondrous land of imagination. Next stop, the Twilight Zone!" Only I don't think I was about to enter another dimension. It was right outside my door and I was stepping in and out of it!

The best explanation I could come up with was that I was experiencing two difference dimensions simultaneously, depending on whether I was outside or inside. I've read about such events since then. Some common denominators seem to be the hazy yellow air, the complete silence, the same structures present although apparently, they were empty, and lack of normal movements like cars driving by, etc.

I was writing this story, when another similar experience resurfaced from the recesses of my mind. It had frightened me so, I guess I tried to forget it. I had gone to the craft store. I was happily pushing my cart in the decorations and candle section. There were some open, free-standing geometrical shelves in that area with lovely, tempting items displayed on them.

I looked in the middle of one of the shelving units. Suddenly, I saw hundreds of that unit forming behind it, as far into infinity as I could see. As I stood in shock at what I was seeing, I looked down and the floor had completely disappeared. I was standing in nothingness, holding on to my shopping cart, and looking through the shelving into hundreds of other dimensions lined up neatly with each other.

I panicked and started gripping the shopping cart handle as hard as I could. I was afraid I might disappear, or fall tumbling into that nothingness. I willed with all of my heart for it to all go away. In a few seconds it did. It was a frightening experience. I wonder, now, if that may be how some people go missing.

In complete fear of the unknown, I put that magic shopping cart right back into the cart corral. I cautiously drove back home with my fingers gripped in fear around the steering wheel. I was praying I it made it to my house instead of arriving in the next galaxy.

I'm sure I experienced a portal and perhaps either accidently opened it, or it opened as I approached. I could have had a marvelous journey, but I wasn't ready to fully step into (cue music) The Twilight Zone.

We aren't really made up of much solid stuff and what seems unbelievable has turned out to be truly possible. It has made me very curious about possibilities. They aren't just in the movies. It can be frightening because most of us have no reference points to weigh against what is happening, but they are real.

Maybe some of what we read or see in movies isn't so preposterous after all. I had forced the phenomenon to stop that day at the craft store. Was it potentially dangerous? Maybe. One event was mildly curious, the other event scared me. I had no idea, and still don't know what might have happened if I had not willed the store back around me and gone home.

Since then, I've heard a man by the name of Jerry Wills, who is a healer and an intuitive, talk about an event that occurred to him. He went through a portal in a rock or rock wall to some other place and time distortion. It's an interesting story. I can't explain it. However, I did see that spy ball fly through my bedroom wall, so there is no doubt in my mind that he could go through rocks under the right circumstance.

Lately, I've sat here writing while my room seems to have been moved somewhere else. The room still exists. It looks a little fuzzy and it feels like it is in some other place, all while I am sitting in it. It's a bit disconcerting. I may have missed out on a terrific experience by not embracing it all, but I just haven't had that much trust. I was still feeling frazzled.

XV

From various classes I've taken, and from participating in various groups and classes online, I have developed friends around the world. We regularly discuss all aspects of spirituality and use our psychic abilities for each other, and to practice and develop. While it's been fun and interesting, it has also added to my skills frazzle, I thought. I was still questioning my true path. My skills were certainly increasing, but they seemed more a pastime, not a direction. Yet, I kept being led to learn about them and, in turn, let to more interesting experiences.

In addition to all of the energy-based certifications I now had, I also picked up a few more in Crystal Healing, Angelic Reiki and Oracle Card reading. I was even an international mentor for intuitive learning to use oracle cards for self-reflection. I was continuing to have amazing experiences, too.

A lady I met through a psychic meetup group (Not the one I was kicked out of) had a crystal collection that made my collection look like the tip of an iceberg. She had the iceberg. She brought some record keeper crystals to a meeting. A record keeper has triangles as inclusions in it. They are believe to hold ancient wisdom. The interesting thing about them was, when I held the crystals, I saw triangles all in them. I handed them to the person sitting next to me who then swore she saw nothing. I took the crystals back and counted the number of triangles I could see out loud. I handed it back. Becoming aggitated, the woman next to me insisted there were no triangles. I even tried to show her the triangles, but she never saw anything there.

I wish I could have spent some time with those crystals. I believe the information was for me to receive and that was why the other person couldn't see the triangles, not even one. Spiritual information can show up in many ways, but we don't always perceive what it may be.

Sometimes I painted or drew spirits I was seeing in my third eye. One was probably me in another life on another planet or realm. As I've already mentioned I had a download from "nowhere" into my head that looked just like the number stream in the movie The Matrix.

I was visiting a friend, Pam. As I walked out of her house to leave for home, I asked Pam if she had ever seen a fairy in her shrubbery. She said, "No." Then, as we stood a couple of feet apart facing each other, a real-live fairy flew up between us for a few seconds. We stared at her. As she began to fly away, Pam excitedly asked, "Did you see that fairy?"

We both saw her in "flesh and blood." We stood there watching as she slowly flew back over to the shrubbery, then up and over the top of the house and away into the sky.

Until that moment, I believed fairies existed. I had experienced them energetically and had seen them with my third eye. I thought they existed in some dimension we didn't. I just didn't know they can be as real as you and I.

My experience with the display shelves at the craft store had convinced me there were far more than seven dimensions. There seemed room for all types of beings existing right along with us, but hidden from our view. My work with energy had convinced me that things can exist in a minut form and take on what we consider normalcy in the right circumstance. I now know, fairies and other beings can be as real as you and me and living right here with us.

In case you are wondering. This fairy looked just like in the books. She was about three inches tall with long brown hair, a short outfit, bare legs and, of course, wings. She flew more like a helicopter than a bird.

I've not seen any other being in my reality yet, just in spirit. After the fairy's appearance, though, I do believe it's possible.

I still didn't know what I was to do with all of these experiences or knowledge. It seems every class I took added a bit more to my repertoire, but not the "one" thing that seemed to be expected, at least by me. No matter what was confirmed spiritually or physically, I just seemed to become more frazzled at each step. I still felt I had no paved or directionally marked path to follow. I wondered, "When am I to become a whole?" I had no idea, but I kept looking for that one thing.

XVI

Certain spiritual channels continued getting much stronger over the years, especially my work with the angels. Unfortunately, I scared one of my clients with an angel. He was about to undergo a heart valve replacement and was having energy work done to be in the best possible health for the surgery. Understandably apprehensive, he asked if I believed in angels. I replied, "I sure do. There is an angel here for you. It's standing right over there in the corner." He flew up from the table, momentarily frightened, because he thought I meant the Angel of Death. I felt terrible. I assured him I had called the angel to help me work on him, and that I always called in angels when I worked on anyone. He settled back down and I continued the work. By the way, his surgery was successful.

 I closed my office and was working for another business when the angels I work with made a big impression on another therapist. As I said, I always asked angels to help me. I left the room where I had been working and another therapist went in. She came running back out in shock. She skidded up to me and stuttered, "Did you just come out of that room?" "Yes," I said. She barely got it out of her mouth, but said, "It's filled with angels!" "I know," I said, "I called them in." Still shocked, she said, "I mean there are a *lot* of them in there--hundreds." Again, I replied, "I always call them in when I'm working." She finally went back into the room, but with caution.

I regularly saw an angel probably twenty feet tall that hung out in the alternative medicine section of the local Borders Book Store. I suppose it was guiding people to the right information.

You've already read about how warrior angels came to protect the preschool and staff where I worked.

XVII

At some point, I noticed that my third eye began to function like a regular eye in addition to functioning psychically. I know that gland has rods and cones just like the two eyes you normally use, but I had been schooled (incorrectly) that it was just a body gland with psychic features.

I had been seeing pictures in my head of things, or people, even short movie-like clips, particularly during readings. That was considered "normal" psychic seeing with your third eye.

I used to see a little preschool aged boy sitting on a simple plank and rope swing that was hung from a tree. He wasn't really swinging, but was staring into a grove of trees a little distance away. I always got the feeling he was waiting for something. What I noticed, too, was how unnaturally vivid green the trees were.

In the movie "What Dreams May Come," the colors of the landscape in heaven are brighter than anything we have here. That's exactly how I saw the colors of the landscape on the plane where the little boy waited. The green of the trees was much more vivid than anything here on earth and hard to describe.

I asked a friend if as a child, he had a swing like the one I saw the little boy sitting on. I thought I was seeing my friend as a little boy. He said, "No," adding that he and his siblings had not had any type of swing. Eventually, I figured out it *was* my friend waiting to come to this life.

I understood my vision of the little boy after I had a conversation with an angel. I had that conversation while receiving a crystal laser treatment from two healers. The angel, I call Robert, and I were standing next to the little boy. The same little boy I saw sitting on the swing. I looked to be 4-5 years old, the boy looked about 3. Robert told me it was time to leave. I hesitated. I was clearly waiting on the little boy, but Robert said that he couldn't come down at the same time as me. I tried to persuade the little boy to come, but the angel was firm with me. I had to go alone. Robert said, "He has to stay with me for a little while. It's time for you to go." When I repeated, "Come on let's go," and tried to wave the little boy forward from where he stood, Robert said more firmly, "No. He has to stay with me for a little while longer. You go on." I reluctantly stepped off into space and twirled down on a twisting rope of energy. I suppose that was when I was born, but I wasn't shown anything else.

I finally understood the connection between the friend and the little boy in the swing when I realized he has the same habit now as an adult. He sits and stares/meditates/thinks while staring into the distance and often into trees. All of that could be written off as psychic in nature but using your third eye can be reality, too.

I found that out my third eye really was a type of eye when it began functioning, or I realized it was, just like my other two eyes. I had a habit of reading for a while before going to sleep. The book usually remained in the bed with me. On many occasions, I have awakened the next morning, picked up the book and started reading again. I would be reading my book and suddenly realize what I was doing. I was reading through my forehead. Apparently, my third eye would fully open during the night and take over for my other two eyes. No wonder my body seemed on hyperalert all night and I had trouble sleeping. My third eye must have been watching everything happening.

After I realized what I was doing, I wouldn't be able to read any more. Then, I would only be able to see with both of my physical eyes until the next time it happened. I have realized I was reading with my third eye numerous times over the past couple of decades. One night, I zoned out and realized I was watching television through my third eye. Of course, it stopped as soon as I realized I was using that eye instead of my other two eyes.

I often wake up with a vivid color picture in my third eye. It is another way I receive spiritual messages. Most of the time I have to figure them out. That's also what I usually have to do when I hear a song in my head over and over. Until I take the time to read the lyrics, I don't usually understand the message I'm being given.

I don't know if the delivery method of messages depends on me, what the information is, or who might be delivering it. I just know there is no one way I receive information. It has always led me to believe I was frazzled. Now, I know better. It is just another filament to light up and adds to my dazzle in the universe.

I've never been much of a dreamer but that seems to be increasing. I seem to have more memories of astral travel than of dreams. In one such memory, I was interacting with a man dressed all in beige. I later got in my car and left his house. He watched as I drove away. I thought it might have been my former father-in-law because he wore khaki work clothes. He wore khaki colored clothes every day that I knew him except for weddings and funerals, and sometimes even then. He had passed away a number of years before this night. He seemed the likely person to be dressed all in beige, or that I might visit on the astral plane.

Months later, I was talking to a psychic friend about the astral travel. She insisted that I knew the man I had driven away from during the astral traveling. She also insisted it wasn't my former father-in-law. I shrugged off her insight and insistence because I couldn't think of anyone else it might be.

In between the traveling dream, and when I talked to my psychic friend about the dream, I met someone while taking photos for the newspaper. I didn't think much about it. He was just in the group of people posing for the photo. I had actually spoken, briefly, to him once before to ask a question about food collections when a disaster struck. I had no idea who he might be, until we were introduced months later.

A few more months went by. I was given some photos of a community event for possible use in the newspaper. Do you want to guess who gave me those photos? I imagine you already have. The man I met while taking photos, gave me the photos of the community event. When he did, I realized he was the man from the astral plane. He was dressed in tan; his uniform!

A couple of years later, I realized I had had an unpleasant encounter with him during a high school football game in a rival town. However, I had never met him until I moved back to my parents' home. When I had encountered him in high school, I was living in my home town. When I met him again, I was living in the town where my parents retired. I think we were destined to meet, somehow, somewhere.

I seem to drive a car often in those other realm visits. I've had my mom and dad hitch a ride in the back seat since they've passed away. I could hear their conversation from the back seat with much more clarity than normal.

During one astral plane drive, I picked up a couple of hitch-hiking buffalo. Yes, they were buffalo who talked and walked on their back legs. As I drove by, they waved me down from the field they stood in, talking. When I stopped, they asked for a ride and climbed into the back seat.

With their skills of persuasion, they convinced me I needed to let them drive my car. I ended up in the back seat while they drove. I don't remember, now, what they told me. As I'm sure you have figured out by now, the buffalo turned out to be spirit guides.

The image of those buffalo driving my car is still pretty funny to me. I suppose that shows how tenaciously I tried to cling to doing things myself. I had learned not to ask for help as a child because it showed weakness. I wasn't likely to get help with anything, anyway. I certainly couldn't image asking a couple of buffalo for help.

I was very resistant to letting my guides take the wheel instead of controlling my own car. It took a bit for the buffalo to convince me that they should be in the driver's seat, not me. They chatted with me about how they could help me, but at that time, it just seemed surreal. Letting my guides completely take the wheel was challenging. Accepting help can still be a struggle.

Now, I don't believe asking for help is weakness, but it was part of my life's conditioning. My dad frequently answered requests for help with, "I don't want to fool with anything for you." I learned not to ask for help as a child. I was often ridiculed if I did. My husband wasn't willing to help with much either.

The buffalo weren't the only animals driving me around at night. A friend had a dog named Magic. His human-like qualities reminded me of that old movie "The Shaggy Dog." He came to visit me in the astral plane a couple of times. During one of those visits he got in my car and started driving it. I have no idea the significance of animals wanting to drive my astral car.

Perhaps, it's just been about letting go and accepting help. The animals were less threatening than a person may have been.

There were other significant events happening that involved mediumship. I didn't realize one particular event was actually showing me that I could be, in fact was, a medium until years later. It took me expanding my definition of what a medium actually was/did to understand I was a medium.

That's important. Don't let what anyone says determine what is true for you. As I said before, conditioning of the mind actually weakens and limits what the spiritual beings can do. We are creators and new things are created every day. Definitions must change by default. It took me years to finally understand that. Don't hang on to what may become an outdated idea that will ultimately hold you back. Now, back to my mediumship experience.

I had a selfcare habit of buying myself a gift for my birthday. That year a local metaphysical shop, near my office, advertised that a lady was coming to the store. She could see and draw spirit guides. The spiritual artist was coming to the store on my birthday. I decided that would be my birthday gift to myself. I had no idea it would be an even bigger gift to my grandparents and an aunt, all of whom had passed away many years before.

As the lady (I wish I remembered her name.) was drawing one of three oriental spiritual medicine men who were guiding me while I facilitated healing in clients, we chatted. She asked me about children and I replied that my children were grown and married. She then asked if I had lost a daughter about 8-10 years old. Although I had lost a son in pregnancy, I had no idea who this girl was. The artist persisted in her questioning, asking if anyone in the family had died at that age. That triggered my memory.

I told her my dad had a sister who passed at about that age. I believed it had been back in the 1930s. The lady asked her name. I replied, "Marian." She then told me, "It's her. When I called the name Marian, she turned and looked at me."

A day or two later, I looked at the family tree. Marian had been seven years old and died in 1936. Marian had passed away nearly sixty years before that day. I had no idea the significance of her appearance or why she would be hanging around looking scared and sad, but she was.

I began to cry huge tears that were running down my face and dripping off my jaw. Alarmed, the artist asked, "Are you okay?" I replied that I was. I wasn't the least bit upset. I knew I was crying, but I was clueless as to why. I was perfectly okay, yet I was crying. There were a lot of really big tears flowing off my face. They began to wet my shirt.

Still alarmed, the lady stopped drawing to inquire about me again. I was still fine, but I told her, "I'm not upset. It looks like I'm standing behind a waterfall of tears, but I'm not upset."

Then the artist informed me that two more spirits had shown

up and were standing on my right side. I realized from her description that they were my paternal grandparents, Marian's parents.

The lady said, "I've got news for you. You just thought you came to have this portrait of spirit guides drawn. You actually came because Marian has been earth bound all this time. She is afraid to go to them. Your grandparents are using you to help her come home."

Marian had died 14 years before I was born. I had heard about her, but had no connection with her that I was aware of. What happened next didn't fit any definition of mediumship I knew. As I mentioned before, be open to definitions evolving in any manner Spirit wishes them to evolve.

The rate of tears falling from my eyes increased as the artist stared at me. I felt energy move through me from my left side. It stopped in the center. I actually felt some hesitation. Then energy moved partially in from the right but then it all moved out through the right side. The tears immediately stopped. I was told Marian had moved through me as her parents reached out to her through me. I had felt it happen while the psychic artist watched it happen. Marian was now with my grandparents who were crying and hugging her. The energy I felt became very light as I was told all three left together. I've never known what those Spirit Tears really were. I don't know if I was expressing their emotions, or somehow, they helped Marion use my energy to return home.

I've learned since then that I was a medium that day. While I don't recommend letting spirits pass through you, apparently it was necessary for Marian. As I've learned more over the years, I've realized that mediumship can come in many forms, not only the version you normally see on television.

Although I have had a couple of other occasions of experiencing "Spirit Tears," as far as I know, I've never been used as a medium in that particular way ever again. Being picked to help an earth-bound spirit return to her loving parents' arms was, and is, an honor to have helped in such an unsuspecting, but beautiful way.

I suspect my grandparents' grief was so strong that it prevented Marian from crossing over. They had done everything possible to save their little girl, even (according to Dad) rounding up five different doctors to treat her. They lived in rural East Texas in a county with less than ten thousand residents. This tragic event took place during the Great Depression when very few people had cars, telephones, even running water. Finding five physicians to come to the aid of their little girl six miles from the nearest town must have been quite a feat of love. She died of pneumonia while the doctors were out in the front yard consulting with each other on how to treat her.

As a young child spirit, sixty years of being earth bound by her parents' loving grief must have been extremely hard for her. It shows how strong love can be and how Spirit will use you for the highest good of all. Just be open to the process and redefining your beliefs instead of following any rule book. Work with your ancestors. You never know what will develop.

As far as I know, I've not had contact with Marian again. I've never seen a photo of her. My grandparents, however, are around watching over and guiding me.

That sounds like a couple of gentle souls, right? Nope, not my grandmother. The past year she has been knocking paintings off the wall just as I was falling sleep. I guess it was the only way she could get my attention, but it sure can keep you awake at night. I asked her to stop, but just a few days before completing this story, she was busy again.

I sat down to look over something on the computer. Just as I sat, I heard this loud paper noise and an 11x14 sheet of paper came floating off the table where it had been for weeks. Despite the loud noise, it gently floated down at my feet. "Hi, Grandma," I said. "Can we find another way to get my attention without you knocking things around?" I will have to wait and see if she gets more subtle!

As you have been reading, things had been evolving all along for me. Some of them were pretty dramatic, but they didn't seem to be very cohesive. I still had a bunch of piles of frazzley stuff instead of one grand plan or path. I was still trying to fit my square peg into well-defined holes of ideology instead of fully letting go and fully trusting. I'm still working on that one, but getting so much closer.

By now you may be wondering when I'm going to get to the point. Frankly, that's exactly what I was wondering, too. I was continuing to question Spirit about that very thing. When, or where is the point? My guidance said, "Keep going with your story."

XVIII

After being literally schooled to choose one path for life, but trying to break free, I found that the metaphysical world was following a lot of organized religion's dogma. In some ways, it began sounding and looking very familiar and I didn't really like the direction things were moving.

I also saw a move to follow a more corporate dogma too, at least in my opinion. The more I studied, the more I saw human placed restrictions. If that works for you, great. As you've been reading, the theme of my life has pretty much been, "Don't fence me in," so it hasn't worked well for me.

All around me, human rules seemed to abound and seemed to grow in number. You can't be performing Reiki on someone if you aren't using the hand symbols and the right protocol for the placement of hands moving down the body. You must shuffle, cut or lay out your cards this way. If you don't do this or that, something horrible will happen or the opposite version; if you do this, something horrible will happen. Trust spirit, but be afraid because there is evil from which you must protect yourself. Be very afraid of a Ouija Board, or pendulums, but cards are okay, or some other version of the same idea, just rotate the tools around in your mind. You have to smudge this way with this thing. You have to walk a certain way for this or that. Sometimes, you were to sacrifice yourself and work for free. None of it was about trusting and working with Spirit, really. There was just a growing set of rules and practice.

Then corporate based methods kicked in even more. I heard or read, you must market and even "go after" people as customers when they are down. Drown them in a media blitz. Give them coupons and special deals. They need you, so go after them. In my imagination, I could just see people running away while screaming, "Leave me alone." This was probably because I became one of them. I felt the industry was moving away from a gentle, loving relationship with Spirit. I didn't want to be subjected to a media blitz focusing on any fears I might have.

In addition, a growing number of people were demanding free energy work and readings because, "It's a gift, so you shouldn't charge me anything." Those same people probably wouldn't give you the shirt off their backs, even if you needed one. They certainly didn't want to pay for what they wanted to consume. I suspect they wouldn't work without receiving a paycheck. It became more and more common, though. It was just another thing distracting from the purpose of such work. Please don't think I'm suggesting practitioners work for free. What I am suggesting is that people demanding a freebie are creating chaos around you and interfering with the true nature of the spiritual work.

The rules and restrictions, and marketing frenzy just seemed to go on and on. There definitely was no certain path to follow, but plenty to choose from and plenty of chaos in every direction. However, much of the classes, training, and opinions offered were still about how to find your true path. Choose one thing (whatever the class was about) and get good at it. Focus, Focus, Focus. All of those opinions just made me think of myself as more frazzled. I was still trying to find my dazzle, no matter how good I became at doing anything.

The idea of "get good at one thing" seemed to be infiltrating every part of the metaphysical world. I began to encounter people who would ask, "What are you?" When I would ask, "What do you mean?" The reply would usually be, "You know what Clair are you?" The person would then rattle off some of the "Clair's" listed here:

Clairvoyance-When you see things like your grandmother who has passed.

Clairaudience-When you hear voices from the other side.

Clairempathy-When you feel what other people feel.

Clairsentence-When you feel energy.

Clairgustance-When you taste things energetically that aren't in your mouth.

Claircognizance-When you just know.

Clairalience/clairolfactant-When you smell things energetically that aren't there.

Clairtangency-When you feel spirits or the energy of objects touch you.

As I considered my answer the first time it happened, I replied, "I am all of those things." I was often scoffed for that answer and told one of my Clair's must be more important than others. It was often accompanied with a distaining vocal tone, and a verbal listing and definition of Clair's as though I was a brain cell or two short, or simply hadn't memorized my homework. However, it was the start of me accepting that spiritual practices are really a package deal. It's all part of the frazzle to dazzle.

How that idea started I have no idea, but I suspect it was people reading on the internet. It sounded like trying to build another corporate model to me. You have to pick one thing and become an expert. Again, trying to split Spiritual skills into compartments just doesn't make sense to me, even after I tried it. If Spirit doesn't communicate in one way, why should I try to receive the messages in just one way, or work with it in one way?

Truly, I hardly ever used just one skill. They switched around or worked in tandem or multiples without me changing a thing consciously. I might touch a client's shoulders and see a toy fire truck. That wasn't using one skill. It was sensing vibration from the client, or around the client, into my hands and transmitting that usually to my third eye. Sometimes, I translated vibration into my psychic ears and I heard a siren, or my physical eyes if I saw a fireman husband standing in spirit in front of us. Just like with our physical bodies, it takes a village of senses to process any vibration into language, whether it be physical or psychic.

Don't fall for the "Be Only One Thing," as I did for a while. As I've been saying, "Spirit's message is to take all the frazzle (different parts of you), light them up, and be the dazzle in your life."

I actually never considered declaring myself just one Clair-something until I was asked. By that time in my life, I wasn't interested in using just one skill. I just couldn't buy the theory that one skill would be my primary anything. The "pick a career" goblin lurked somewhere in the dark corners of my mind, though.

From that old childhood conditioning of trying to get things right, I did some self-doubting. Maybe I did need to pick one thing and stick to it? I spent a lot of money and time studying while attempting to figure out what my true path was. I suppose deep inside I wanted to hold some sort of title that declared me good enough. As you know, what I got, instead, was a whole lot of confusion and frazzled intention, but I also got a whole lot better at all of it. There began to be a whole lot more pieces with which to work. So, I turned more and more to what felt right to me and what I was being told by my GPS-Guidance for my Personal Soul.

Unless life was preordained and the Universe didn't need variety to evolve, claiming to use just one area of sensing just didn't add up. I knew that wasn't true. The Universe changes all of the time. Astronomers frequently discover new stars, solar systems and black holes. Here on Earth, flora and fauna change, disappear and new things suddenly appear seemingly out of nowhere. To me, it just didn't make sense to be, *only*, the one thing you thought of at five years old or even seventeen years old. There is so much more to life. Why would it make sense in the other areas of your life?

The Universe was designed to change and mutate in a variety of ways for people like you and me. The ones Spirit created to look at the world a bit differently. You know, the outsiders who wear polka dots in a follow-the-leader beige world. The soul who wonders what would happen if a kaleidoscope became a movie projector and if you could then dance through the colors into another world. It's for the ones who say, I wonder if..." and a real-life fairy appears or a loved one from the other side drops a dime at their feet. It takes imagination and being open. It's about working with God, Spirits, Angels, and your higher self. It's about being God-like, co-creating and making something new, different and probably improved. As some ads on television declare, I found out, "God approves this message."

XIX

I was sitting outside and being quiet. I decided to talk to God instead of just waiting for a word or two from "anyone" up there. In the midst of our talk, God said, "You know, Lillie, you make me smarter." That took some contemplation. Wouldn't that mean I was expanding, even challenging God, by changing myself or changing things around me? As I mulled it over, I realized that is exactly what takes place. Each new thought or deed creates a reaction somewhere in the energy field and shakes the matrix. The entire matrix then responds, not just within or around me. So, then what happens?

Well, God, Goddess, Spirit, whatever name you use, then looks at what you just did or thought, and responds. If it was your seeing or thinking something entirely new from crashing a couple of brain cells together, God says, "I don't know how she managed to do that, but let's see what I think about that, or what I can do with it, or about it.

God's Energy Team is always on alert because, with Free Will, it doesn't know exactly how you will respond. It tweaks itself in response, just as much, or more, than you tweak your response to events. From those subtle, or great shifts in being, evolution happens. Each time there is a change in us, we move up the spiral a little closer to God. Even ideas that don't work out still cause change, and our being grows and evolves.

It happens when people exchange ideas, or your pet challenges you to develop an escape proof place because all the other containment ideas didn't work. It happens when a strip of land is paved and a tree grows in a crack that opened up, or those yellow flowers suddenly throw off a purple bloom. Spirit works in creative, ingenious, and miraculous ways and in it's interaction with us.

Those changes don't just result in evolution. They stand as ways to bridge the gap between our human existence and the Universal Realms. When we connect to the spirit of trees, or the great horned owl, the fairies, or the beauty of wildflowers, we are connecting to the God Spirit in all things, and it sets up spiritual connections and communication. We also speak to each other in spiritual ways without realizing it. We speak through vibration and often without words. Through our thoughts, actions, maturation, and evolution, transformation takes place. We make each other smarter. We make God and the Universe smarter. We are much more important in the scheme of things than we might have been taught to believe. Each of us is needed to make the world and the universe go around and get better.

There is no right or wrong way. There are ideas that work and ideas that don't. Then, there are just ways we do things. The Bible says, "There is no monotony in the workmanship of God." All we have to do is seek and seek in our own way. Just find what interests you and what feels natural to you. As you work with it, bam! You get smarter and God gets smarter.

If you heard a litany of, "You're not pretty enough. You're not smart enough, or popular, or talented enough. Even, you are worthless and no good," like I did. It's past time to forget those words. Let them dissolve into the floor, or up into the sky. Let them go. Don't give them the energy to stay alive in your life. You are none of those things. The people who told you such things are simple blinded and jealous of your dazzle.

Step into what you have passion for and co-create, co-create, co-create. If you don't know what that might be, look at what

God has been dangling in front of your nose. It took me decades to finally understand I was to translate light into the vibration of words and color. It was there all along, I was just looking in other directions.

While my life has been filled with disappointments, rejection, fear, anxiety, low self-esteem, and physical and emotional paint, it's still been filled with fun, laughter, love, and a lot of learning and growing. It's been filled with all sorts of communication from Spirit, whether or not, I was listening and responding.

I've still been putting one foot in front of the other and trying. That's it. I was trying. By trying, I was changing. I was adding filaments to the fiber and making the rope to climb even higher. It took quite a while to understand that there is a better view from up there, though. I'm still working on integrating it into my being.

While I can see it now, I was often swinging for the fence. I couldn't see the fence, though and that, apparently, was right where Spirit wanted me. I didn't understand it because I wasn't fully trusting. It took a message that said, "Look in your peripheral vision where nothing is formed yet," for me to understand it was ok to bat at things I didn't know, couldn't see, or understand as enlightening. It wasn't about coming apart, but taking the parts and adding them together.

XX

Conclude, but don't stop. Accept and assess, but don't define. Don't check off boxes of events, or characteristics of what you think you need to do, have, or be. Have no expectations. Allow yourself to grow into something you can't imagine. Have fuzzy edges when you make plans, or start something new. That way, Spirit can surprise you with something greater than you have imagined.

Not everyone is wired to be open or optimistic. Not everyone is programmed to accept being in the flow in his/her own unique way. However, everyone can do it in some way. You just have to allow your soul to speak its language, *not* a programmed language.

Many of us carry backpacks full of karmic and family wounds. We have experiences that make us feel unsafe. We close down to spiritual communication and love because we don't remember what unconditional love feels like, or sounds like. We may have had no examples here in our physical life to help us remember that unconditional love we felt when originating from the Higher Being.

For most of us, one of the first words we heard frequently was, "No." As I mulled that over, I realized that could be the true veil of forgetfulness. Those two letters could be what shuts down our memory of pure unconditional love. In just a few months, we are conditioned to abandon curiosity and experiential learning whether that be in the physical world or the spiritual world.

We are taught to fear instead of facing life with an open heart. We forget our innate intelligence and abilities. We are taught to believe in the finite, not possibilities. We are taught to listen to people instead of to our soul. Unfortunately, people often want to put obstacles in place to make us stop whatever we are doing. Our expansion makes them uncomfortable and they don't want to adjust. It's not because there might be something wrong within us, or something evil about what we do.

I received a message a few months before starting this story. It was, "Stop using the word block. There is no such thing. You are simply being asked to take smaller steps." That was it. Don't believe in blocks that prevent you from achieving what you want to achieve.

I was told by my guidance not to believe in the finite. I was to believe, only, that moving in varying degrees, or steps, could help me reach toward possibility, and even beyond what I could imagine. I was instructed to place no limits on any word, thought, or action that might plant itself into the process. Actually, that's quite a challenge. Moving from all of the conditioning most of us have had means letting go of the non-belief in magical, spiritual happenings.

I was instructed to let go of words and their definitions, and to simply process expanding energy. It's a bit mind-exploding to think about trying to let go of actual words, but they have limits to their vibration. It's a step down from the spiritual vibration when we actually hear a word.

It isn't about thinking your way through something, but allowing it all to flow and vibrate inside and all around you. Then allow it to escape from you and see what *it* wants to be, rather than containing it as a word or definition. It's also about allowing it to boomerang back at you and possibly take on another form.

It isn't about trying to be one-size-fits-all. It's about letting the frazzle parts dazzle. The more pieces you imagine and accept as "lit up," the more you will *DAZZLE!*

As you've read, I'm no different from anyone. I often want clear answers. I just have to remember-it's better if I allow the answers to be more than what *I* imagined.

The Spiritual World gets to choose how it speaks to us, just like you get to choose the words and body language you use when communicating with anyone. So, let your soul choose its language. Whether it's putting dots on a rock, grilling, painting, building houses, or channeling archangels, Spirit has a way it wants to communicate with you. Allow that.

I just chose the random examples above, but think about how those might be put together. Better yet, allow those things to work together to bring a message to yourself or others. You will be surprised what happens. Little bits of frazzle matter.

The Spiritual and Physical Worlds get to choose when and where we get a message, just like you choose the right moment to speak to someone. We just have to be ready because the different worlds are speaking to us all of the time. We just don't pick up most of the vibration.

I may have to wait. You may have to wait. Sometimes I've already gotten an answer. Then, something happens, or someone says something and I think, "Oh right, I heard that, or I saw that coming." Guidance is there, always. We just don't pay enough attention to what is available.

We never have to go it alone, regardless of what our life might have been. People, messages, events, even animals arrive in our lives in what seems to be random ways, but it's not.

While writing this book, I received a message to hang up my coat of identity. Then I started hearing Dolly Parton's song, "A Coat of Many Colors." I was puzzled about that for a few hours and then, tah-dah, I realized Spirit was affirming what I've been writing about.

Take off the one thing (coat) and see yourself as those many colors. Spirit was rephrasing, "<u>Let Your Frazzle Be Your Dazzle</u>." How great is that? It also repeated a message I received one day while painting, "Translate the light into vibration and color." For me that means translate how I receive Spirit into words and colorful creations.

Nothing is random, no more than your frazzle is random. Not even hearing about a colorful coat is random. It all brings a new awareness and new opportunities to add another filament that can light up the Universe with your *DAZZLE*.

I had filed away many events in my memory before starting this writing process. Writing this life review revived them.

While my life has been filled with disappointments, rejection, fear, anxiety, low self-esteem and physical and emotional pain, it's also been filled with all the crazy, funny and miraculous things you've read and many more.

Now that I look back, every single thing was important in some way. I don't believe that every painful event is a lesson, and certainly not punishment. Pain can be a learning platform to build upon and to bring in other things, that build into something really big and dazzling.

Some events of my life took over a half a century to realize that some good had come from some of the pain. I had to learn new terms and allow new definitions. I had to have other experiences. I sometimes had to compile things over a number of years before I found a use for it, whether that be helping people, or listening to a message that saved my life.

There were events that taught me to consciously change family patterns. Some things taught me to see my life as more miraculous than I believed it to be. Even some of the horrific events have had serendipitous results. I've learned how to help people heal their wounds because I've had those wounds, and I've worked to heal from them. Spirit has been beside me every step of the way whether I realized it or not.

Think of the times you wondered why you were doing something, or you had a sudden compulsion to go to a place you've never been before. Why did you feel a need to study that particular subject? When you look at what seems to be mounting frazzle, look for the connecting dots and spiritual action within those events, people, messages, even animal behavior. I promise those things are there, and have happened to make your *DAZZLE* brighter. You are becoming blindingly bright where it counts. You are dazzling the Spiritual Realms. You are seen. You are somebody special!

The Universe is waiting for you to realize you've been tuned in all along. Allow yourself to be open to the unknown. Let go of preconceptions of how Spirit should look and interact with you. Open your heart to the possibility of you. There is *DAZZLE* waiting to burst forth.

Spirit likes to have fun with us. If your life isn't much fun, stick with Spirit. The Universe will make you laugh, wrap you in a warm hug and whisper in your ears, or show you in a myriad of ways just how truly fantastic God thinks you are.

On a day when I wasn't feeling very in love with my life, I asked for this message. I wanted to see the word believe someplace. I drove to get my car inspected and afterwards pulled into a fast-food drive-through. In front of me was a car whose license plate read "BLV." I laughed and said, "Thanks! I get it!"

Sometimes your spiritual posse plays with you just so you remember they are there. When something silly happens, I just say, "Very funny." While I might not get their sense of humor, I fully understand there is more to this life than meets the eye and they are reminding me of that fact, especially through synchronicities that are too obvious to ignore.

I visited the Texas Quilt Museum. As I stood by the Visitor Sign In Book, I was telling a friend about how my great aunt had made a quilt for my high school graduation. A lady walked up and signed the book just before me. Her last name was Senn. The maiden name of my great aunt and an unusal name in this state. Coincidence? I don't think so.

Another time, I started creating a gift certificate graphic. The phone rang right after I started. A lady was calling to request a gift certificate for a newspaper subscription.

Pay attention. Those synchronicities happen all the time when Spirit wants you to know it's around, or to pay speciall attention to something.

I hope I've inspired you to look back through your life and find the crazy, awesome, and miraculous things you may have experienced. Don't worry about what you might find, or if you will find something. Just get started. I promise you've had spiritual experiences, too.

Your experiences probably won't be like mine, but you've had them. That is the beauty of reviewing the events of your life. Ferret out those bits you think are frazzled and accept them as dazzling bits of a whole you. Spirit doesn't choose "special" people to help. It chooses everyone, even you!

There is no conundrum. God doesn't end where we begin. Nor do we end where God begins, because Spirit doesn't end. So, why try to live your life that way? Let your soul speak its language whatever that vibration may be.

I met someone who told me about putting dots on rocks. She said children always show up whenever she is doing her dotting. She looked at me and said, "Lillie, they are just dots on rocks." Clearly, there was more to it than she was recognizing. The point is, whether it's putting dots on rocks, or trimming trees to the perfect shape, allow your soul to speak its language.

I didn't realize I had been living a life by conclusion because I was so busy trying to stuff myself inside a preconceived box. I had a foot in each world trying to fit in, yet I was trying to expand out of the box. Once I stopped trying to reach conclusions mentally, physically or spiritually, it was easier to see that many of the events in my life were the result of Divine Guidance, and they could be used in a variety of ways. I didn't have to grab the brass ring to be accepted, I could just ride the merry-go-round and have a great time. So, give a queen wave (Even if you are a guy). *DAZZLE!*

The things that might not have been part of the original Divine Plan (We do have free will.) have been put to purposeful use, even if it took years to accomplish. Just think about the hoops Spirit jumped through to finally get me to begin a writing career. Spirit is, if anything, persistent and allowing. We are allowed opportunity after opportunity to understand how to *DAZZLE*.

I'm not even close to completing my spiritual growth. I don't think we are until we reach that state of I AM. That's okay, though. We are called here because our experiences can help, not only ourselves, but others as well. We are called here to make everything and everyone smarter, including ourselves, and God.

As I was working on the illustrations for this book, I had an experience I have never had before. My left ear started vibrating so strongly it was making a noise. It felt completely different afterwards, like it was bigger, but yet more loosely formed.

I turned to my spiritual guidance and asked, "What the heck just happened?" I was told, "You ear was just attuned to a high frequency. You will begin to receive much more telepathy than you already do. Then, I heard that same voice query, "You are open to all forms of communication, correct?"

I had been saying I was open to all forms of communication for several weeks while I was trying to clear some energetic clogging of my ears. Obviously, I was taken seriously. I'm happy for that. It was just surprising how it happened. I listened to guidance to create illustrations and that led to something greater I hadn't imagined. I was translating Light into color and illustrations to help tell my story.

I was next told, "Just know that there is no path. There is only you taking evolving and expanding twists, turns, loops, bypasses-even sidesteps."

Later that night, I felt what seemed to be bubbles about the size of marbles exploding around the circle of my crown chakra. Was that another form of communicating? I have no idea. I was so busy paying attention to how it felt and the pattern it was making, I failed to see if I could get a message from the bubbles.

As the bubbles happened a couple of hours after my ear started vibrating and getting bigger energetically, I believe it probably was just another way the spiritual world was communicating. Maybe it was a moment of connecting to dolphins. I have no idea, but I am open to possibility. While I may not have consciously picked up on a message, I do believe we absorb the vibrations of information in many ways. If we don't hear or see the guidance, that's okay too. It's still there. It's possible to simply absorb guidance.

My guidance had reminded me of what I had been saying, "I am open to all forms communication." I have to trust that my soul knows, hears, sees, feels, and that it has the ability to decode, process, and retain that vibration as something useful, and, maybe, profound for the world. It has its language to speak.

We just never know what or how the Spiritual Universe is going to speak to us. I seem to receive messages differently each time, more often than I receive messages in the same way. It's never a dull moment.

It's very appropriate for me. I get bored easily and like to change things about. Don't you suppose the Universe knows this? I just didn't realize how well it knew me. That boredom, though, really means I'm ready to change and grow some more. It my job to allow Spirit to change me.

If you don't see the whole enchilada, it's okay. I rarely do either. I receive bits and pieces and then I must take the ingredients, stir them together, roll them up and slap on some sauce myself to get the entire message, or to benefit from the process.

Even in this book, you can read where I am still getting messages as I write about the topic. Spirit tweaks us as we grow and change.

My spiritual guidance, even in bits and pieces, is also my constant teacher. It pushes continually to expand my awareness and yours does, too. In order for there to be no resistance and so that new things and experiences can form, I try to remember to have fuzzy edges while tapping into my awareness. That's how I, and you, can become more dazzling than our wildest dreams.

That's why I wrote my story. I'm not complete. I have not finished expanding and growing. What seemed to leave me a frazzled mess actually gave me more filaments to light up. Spirit wanted me to know I could light up a room. God wanted me to know he believes in me.

Spirit wants you to know you aren't complete either. That's exactly how you are supposed to be, a jack of all spiritual trades.

I thought I was seeking a path, but I was really trying on new things right and left and creating that coat with all the colors. I was exercising and flexing muscles I didn't know I had, or could use.

I've realized I'm not really frazzled. I grow stronger each and every time I try something new. Even when an experience seems weird, crazy, or humbling, I am a sparkler that grows brighter every day.

If you think you've never had an experience with spiritual interaction, think of a time when you avoided something horrific because you kept losing your keys like I did. Maybe you just missed a car chase going through an intersection because your toddler fell out in a tantrum and it took that extra five minutes to get him into the car seat. I promise...your spiritual moments are there, even in the smallest of ways and in big ways, too. They may be passing by while you aren't paying attention, or resisting the messages, just like I did for so long.

I've said this before. Spirit declares, "There is no frazzle." Stop judging yourself. You aren't the opinion of others, or of yourself. You aren't a lowly, ugly, untalented, undesirable, or whatever else other people, or you, may have used to describe yourself.

Stop parroting other's words and making them your own nega-

tive self-talk. It's your opinion of you that makes up the who
you, so light that fire! *DAZZLE!*

If it seems hard to get started, you feel like you are stuck in neutral, or if you feel whipped by life, I get it. A life review like this one can bring things into perspective. It doesn't matter if you feel like you are on a path you didn't choose. Let me remind you-there is no path and Spirit is your walking stick to support you.

Every place you have wandered; everything you have done, or wanted to do, has been a process of discovery and growth. If you have responded to Spiritual guidance, if you *really* look, you can see where you have expanded. If not, it's never too late and a life review can help you do that.

I saw that I had been on a journey. I saw that I had been responding to Spiritual guidance, whether it had been a clear turn right at the next intersection, losing my keys to save my life, or being shown that fairies can be real.

In some ways, I limited my options by trying too hard to be the explorer. I asked for specific things in specific ways in an attempt to control the outcome. Sometimes, I then wished I hadn't gotten what I had asked for because something better could have come into my life.

I have doubted myself because I was afraid-afraid I wouldn't be good enough. I know now, it was the fear that I was unlovable that haunted me, not that I wasn't on the right journey.

I had been asking for what I thought I wanted for a long time, "Show me the way I am to go." I finally heard my answer through the filters of my life. I am okay. Spirit wants to use me just as I am because I am not frazzled, I am a dazzling beacon to light the way for others.

After I heard the phrase that day, "Let your frazzle be your dazzle," I knew why I kept hearing messages to, "Just wait. It's coming." I had to be in the right frame of mind and being, to finally let go and tell my story. I was given a flash of light through the mes-

ee my own light. That included a vision of a very
er.

ays loved sparklers! It's no wonder that Spirit provided
age for me. Sparklers are dazzling., but they aren't comprised of one thing. The pieces don't burn at the same time. They
don't burn with the same intensity. Still, when it all starts to
burn, it is a dazzling thing of beauty.

The more bits there are to catch that spiritual fire, the brighter
it shines. Just like me. Just like you. We are all sparklers. The more
seemingly frazzled bits of our spiritual selves there are to catch
fire, the brighter we shine throughout the Universe. Embrace
those bits and pieces. They aren't separate, they are tied together
with spiritual energy.

It took all of these experiences and more to light up my soul in
ways I might not have pursued otherwise. My life may have left
some of me shattered, but I am not broken. It took a lifetime for
me to finally stop holding on so tightly to myself, trembling in
fear that I was unlovable, and to trust that I might have *DAZZLE*.

Look over your life. Have you been dreaming of possibilities?
That's a start. Have you been exploring possibilities even if it
ended in an epic fail? That's beneficial frazzle! You just never
know how that might turn into a message that sends you up into a
more brilliant version of you.

Before my painting changed to a spiritual co-creation, I was
trying for perfection and often failed. I had a stack of canvases in
the corner that I eventually started painting over.

I decided one day I wanted to paint something happy. I decided
on a happy Buddha. Spirit and I got started co-creating. After I
finished the painting, I realized that the Buddha's face actually
makes a heart, a loving message for everyone to see.

Another canvas I turned a different direction and started an
entirely different subject matter. Some of the old painting was
showing through. I decided to leave it. It added some beneficial

dimension to the painting. I did a couple more like that, turning them a different direction, and allowing part of the old painting to show through. They turned out beautifully.

Spirit was giving me a lesson that the old stuff you've done, or experienced, can be co-created into something more beautiful in the future. It's my story and I am free to add a plot twist to my life whenever I feel like it. So, allow for your possibilities and spiritual possibilities, rather than conclusion.

Now when I go somewhere, I'm not going to worry about dimming my light to make others comfortable. I'm not going to worry about all the bits and pieces. It's more important to be true to myself and true to how my spiritual guidance wants me to develop. I am taking Spirit's advice and I hope you do too. _"Let Your Frazzle Be Your Dazzle!_

ACKNOWLEDGEMENT

To the sometimes elusive, often startling, always supportive, knowledgeable, wacky and entertaining spiritual beings who share the universe with me: Without you, life would seem boring and I might be considered normal.

To Kay Shearer: Who knows I'm not normal and accepts me anyway, even when llamas fly in the middle of the night.

To the Eyerollers in my life: At least I can see you are listening.

ABOUT THE AUTHOR

Lillie Ruby

A Native Texan, Lillie Ruby grew up in a small ranching and gas field community where she began learning to translate the vibration of Spiritual Light into words and color. A former journalist, and now author, artist and Spiritual Light Translator, Lillie has been honored with numerous Texas Press Association Awards. She also received a Freedom of Speech Award and other Honorary Awards for her work with governmental entities, school districts and civic organizations.

Lillie earned a BS in Education from Stephen F. Austin State University, where she was inducted into Phi Kappa Delta Honorary Fraternity. She earned an Early Childhood Certification from the University of Houston. Lillie also earned an AA in Applied Sciences/Massage Therapy from Heritage College where she received the Director's Award for Academic Excellence.

After founding and operating several private preschools, Lillie served as a Volunteer Trainer for the Mid-West Center for Nonprofit Leadership Director's Institutes. She worked in the field of domestic violence as a Social Worker with young children and served as Co-Chair of the Educational Committee for the Kansas City Area Coalition to educate the legal and law enforcement community on the effects of domestic violence on children. She served for several years as a validator for the Accreditation Program under the National Association for the Education of the Young Child, and as a Trainer for a national child-care company.

Lillie earned a National Certification in Massage Therapy and is Certified in Usui Reiki, Angel Reiki, Matrix Energetics, Sound Therapy, Crystal Healing, Spiritual Response Therapy, Space Clearing, Cranial Sacral Therapy and Touch Healing. She has also studied Emotional Freedom Techniques (EFT). Lillie is a Certified Oracle Guide and served as a Mentor for the Collette Baron-Reid Oracle School. Lillie is also certified as an Angel Tarot Reader by Radleigh Valentine. She is a personal coach using the INvison process. Lillie also studied under many famous names in the fields of mediumship and sound healing.

Active in her community, Lillie trained to be a member of the local Citizens Emergency Response Team and is a member of the Waller County Recovery Committee. Lillie is also a Master Gardener.

The photo shows Lillie Ruby at about age 3. You can see spirit faces in the shrub and a spirit guide in the upper right hand corner. After finding this photo of herself, Lillie knew that she had been in contact with spirits all of her life.

DAZZLE

IS

MY FAVORITE COLOR

Made in the USA
Middletown, DE
13 April 2021